True Words for Brave Men

A Book for Soldiers' and Sailors' Libraries

Charles Kingsley

True Words for Brave Men: A Book for Soldiers' and Sailors' Libraries

The present edition is a reproduction of previous publication of this classic work. Minor typographical errors may have been corrected without note; however, for an authentic reading experience the spelling, punctuation, and capitalization have been retained from the original text.

ISBN: 979-8-88830-958-2

Dedicated

By Kind Permission
to
General Sir William Codrington, G.C.B.,
and
Admiral Wellesley, C.B.,
in memory of
Charles Kingsley,
who was proud of their friendship,
and loved and honoured them
as he loved and honoured
all brave soldiers
and sailors.

"Yet was he courteous still to every wight,
And loved them that did to armes incline."
Spenser

CONTENTS

Part II

INTRODUCTORY NOTE

This little volume is selected from the unpublished sermons and addresses of Charles Kingsley by the request of a Colonel of Artillery, and with the sanction of an Army Chaplain of long experience, who knew the influence of his writings on soldiers, and who wish that that influence may live, though he is no longer here. The Lecture on Cortez was given at Aldershot Camp in 1858, and the Address to Brave Soldiers and Sailors written for and sent out to the troops before Sebastopol in the winter of 1855, when Mr. Kingsley's own heart, with that of all England, was grieving over the sufferings of our noble army in the Crimea. F. E. K.

I

THE GOOD CENTURION

OR

THE MAN UNDER AUTHORITY

"And when Jesus was entered into Capernaum, there came unto Him a centurion, beseeching Him and saying, Lord, my servant lieth at home, sick of the palsy, grievously tormented. And Jesus said unto him, I will come and heal him. The centurion answered and said, Lord, I am not worthy that Thou shouldest come under my roof: but speak the word only, and my servant shall be healed. For I am a man under authority, having soldiers under me, and I say unto this man, Go, and he goeth; and to another, Come, and he cometh; and to my servant, Do this, and he doeth it. When Jesus heard it, he marvelled, and said to them that followed, Verily I say unto you, I have not found such great faith, no, not in Israel."—
Matt. viii. 5-10.

We find in Holy Scripture, that of the seven heathens who were first drawn to our Lord Jesus Christ and His gospel, three were soldiers.

The first was the Centurion, of whom our Lord speaks in such high terms of commendation.

The next, the Centurion who stood by His cross, and said, "Truly this was the son of God." Old legends say that his name was Longinus, and tell graceful tales of his after-life, which one would fain believe, if there were any evidence of their truth.

The third, of course, was Cornelius, of whom we read in the Acts of the Apostles.

Now these three Centurions—commanding each a hundred men—had probably risen from the ranks; they were not highly educated men; they had seen endless cruelty and immorality; they may have had, at times, to do ugly work themselves, in obedience to orders. They were doing, at the time when they are mentioned in

Scripture, almost the worst work which a soldier can do. For they were not defending their own country against foreign enemies. They were keeping down a conquered nation, by a stern military despotism, in which the soldiery acted not merely as police, but as gaolers and executioners. And yet three men who had such work as this to do, are singled out in Scripture to become famous through all time, as the first-fruits of the heathen; and of one of them our Lord said, "I have not found such great faith, no, not in Israel."

Why is this? Was there anything in these soldiers' profession, in these soldiers' training, which made them more ready than other men to acknowledge the Lord Jesus Christ? And if so; what was it?

Let us take the case of this first Centurion, and see if it will tell us. We will not invent any reasons of our own for his great faith. We will let him give his own reasons. We will let him tell his own story. We may trust it; for our blessed Lord approved of it. Our Lord plainly thought that what the soldier had spoken, he had spoken well. And yet it is somewhat difficult to understand what was in his mind. He was plainly no talker; no orator. Like many a good English soldier, sailor, yeoman, man of business, he had very sound instincts in him, and drew very sound conclusions from them: but he could not put them into words. He knew that he was right, but he could not make a speech about it. Better that, than be—as too many are—ready to make glib speeches, which they only half believe themselves; ready to deceive themselves with subtle arguments and high-flown oratory, till they can give the most satisfactory reasons for doing the most unsatisfactory and unreasonable things. No, the good soldier was no orator: but he had sound sense under his clumsy words. Let us listen to them once more.

"I am a man under authority, having soldiers under me. And I say to this man, Go, and he goeth; and to another, Come, and he cometh; and to my servant, Do this, and he doeth it." Surely the thought which was in his mind is to be found in the very words which he used—Authority. Subordination. Discipline. Obedience. He was under authority, and must obey his superior officer. He had soldiers under him, and they must obey him. There must be not only no mutiny, but no neglect, no arguing, no asking why. If he said Go, a man must go; if he said Come, a man must come; and make no words about it. Otherwise the Emperor's service would go to ruin, through laziness, distrust, and mutinous talk. By subordination, by discipline, by mutual trust and strict obedience, that empire of Rome was conquering the old world; because every Roman knew his place, and every Roman did what he was told.

But what had that to do with our Lord's power, and with the healing of the child?

This. The honest soldier had, I think, in his mind, that subordination was one of the most necessary things in the world; that without it the world could not go on. Then he said to himself, "If there must be subordination on earth, must there not be subordination in heaven?" If he, a poor officer, could get his commands obeyed, by merely speaking the word; then how much more could God. If Jesus was—as He said—as His disciples said—the Lord, the God of the Jews: then He had no need to come and see a sick man; no need to lay His hands on him; to perform ceremonies or say prayers over him. The Laws of Nature, by which health and sickness come, would obey His word of command without rebellion and without delay. "Speak the word only, Lord, and my servant shall be healed."

But how did the Centurion know—seemingly at first sight, that Jesus was the Lord God? Ah, how indeed?

I think it was because he had learnt the soldier's lesson. He had seen many a valiant officer—Tribunes, Prefects, Consuls, Emperors, commanding men; and fit to command men. There was no lack of such men in the Roman empire then, as the poor, foolish, unruly Jews found out to their cost within the next forty years. And the good Centurion had been accustomed to look at such men; and to look up to them beside, and say not merely—It is a duty to obey these men, but—It is a delight to obey them. He had been accustomed—as it is good for every man to be accustomed—to meet men superior to himself; men able to guide and rule him. And he had learned—as every good soldier ought to learn—when he met such a man, not to envy him, not to backbite him, not to intrigue against him, not to try to pull him down: but to accept him for what he was—a man who was to be followed, if need be, to the death.

There was in that good Centurion none of the base spirit of envy, which dreads and therefore hates excellence, hates ability, hates authority; the mutinous spirit which ends, not—as it dreams—in freedom and equality, but in slavery and tyranny; because it transforms a whole army—a whole nation—from what it should be, a pack of staunch and faithful hounds, into a mob of quarrelsome and greedy curs. Not of that spirit was the good Centurion: but of the spirit of reverence and loyalty; the spirit which delights in, and looks up to, all that is brave and able, great and good; the spirit of true independence, true freedom, and the true self-respect which respects its fellow men; and therefore it was, that when the Centurion came into the divine presence of Christ, he knew at once, instinctively and by a glance, into what a presence he had come.

Christ's mere countenance, Christ's mere bearing, I believe, told that good soldier who He was. He knew of old the look of great commanders: and now he saw a countenance, in spite of all its sweetness, more commanding than he had ever seen before. He knew of old the bearing of Consuls and of Emperors: and now, in spite of Christ's lowly disguise, he recognised the bearing of an Emperor of emperors, a King of kings. He had learnt of old to know a man when he met one; and now, he felt that he had met the Man of all men, the Son of Man; and that so God-like was His presence, that He must be likewise the Son of God.

And so had this good soldier his reward; his reward for the soldierly qualities which he had acquired; for subordination; for reverence; for admiration of great and able men. And what was his reward? Not merely that his favourite servant was healed at his request: but that he learnt to know the Lord Jesus Christ, whom truly to know is everlasting life; whom the selfish, the conceited, the envious, the slanderous, the insolent, the mutinous, know not, and never will know; for they are not of His Spirit, neither is He of theirs.

But more: What is the moral which old divines have drawn from this story? "If you wish to govern: learn first to obey." That is a moral lesson more valuable than even the use of arms. To learn—as the good Centurion learnt—that a free man can give up his independence without losing it. Losing it? Independence is never more called out than by subordination. A man never feels himself so much of a free man as when he is freely obeying those whom the laws of his country have set over him. A man never feels so able as when he is following the lead of an abler man than himself. Remember this. Make it a point of honour to do your duty earnestly, scrupulously, and to the uttermost; and you will find that the habits of self-restraint, discipline, and obedience, which you, as soldiers, have learned, will stand you in good stead for the rest of your lives, and make you each, in his place, fit to rule, just because you have learned to obey.

But now go on a step, as the good Centurion went on, and say—If there is no succeeding in earthly things, whether in soldiering or any other profession, without subordination; without obeying rules and orders strictly and without question: then perhaps there is no succeeding in spiritual and heavenly things. For has not God His moral Laws, His spiritual Laws, which must be obeyed, if you intend to prosper in this life, or in the life to come?

"Thou shalt love the Lord thy God with all thy heart and soul, and thy neighbour as thyself. Thou shalt honour thy father and thy mother. Thou shalt not kill, steal, commit adultery, slander, or covet." So it is written: not merely on those old tables of stone on Sinai; but in The Eternal Will of God, and in the very nature of this world, which God has made. There is no escaping those Laws. They fulfil themselves. God says to them, "Go," and they go; "Come," and they come; "Do justice on the offender," and they do it. If we are fools and disobey them, they will grind us to powder. If we are wise and obey them, they will reward us. For in wisdom's right hand is length of days, and in her left hand riches and honour. Her ways are ways of pleasantness, and all her paths are peace. She is a tree of life to them that lay hold of her, and blessed is every one that retaineth her; as God grant you all will do.

But you, too, in time may have soldiers under you. Think, I beseech you, earnestly of this, and for their sake, as well as for your own, try by God's help to live worthy of Christian English men. Let them see you going out and coming in, whether on duty or by your own firesides, as men who feel that they are "ever beneath their great taskmaster's eye;" who have a solemn duty to perform, namely, the duty of living like good men toward your superior officers, your families, your neighbours, your country, and your God—even towards that Saviour who so loved you that He died for you on the cross, to set you the example of what true men should be; the example of perfect duty, perfect obedience, perfect courage, perfect generosity—in one word—the example of a perfect Hero.

Live such lives, and then, will be fulfilled to you, and to your children after you, from generation to generation, the promises which God made, ages since, to the men of Judea of old; promises which are all true still, and will continue true, in every country of the world, till the world's end.

"Put thou thy trust in the Lord, and be doing good; dwell in the land, and verily thou shalt be fed.

The Lord knoweth the doings of the righteous; and their inheritance shall endure for ever.

They shall not be confounded in the perilous time; and in the days of dearth they shall have enough.

The Lord ordereth a good man's going; and maketh his way acceptable to himself.

Though he fall, he shall not be cast down; for the Lord upholdeth him with his hand.

I have been young, and now I am old; yet saw I never the righteous forsaken, nor his seed begging their bread.

Flee from evil, and do the thing that is good; and dwell for evermore.

For the Lord loveth the thing that is right; He forsaketh not his that are godly, but they are preserved for ever." Amen.

II

CHRIST IS COME. A CHRISTMAS SERMON

"For unto us a child is born, unto us a son is given: and the government shall be upon his shoulder: and his name shall be called Wonderful, Counsellor, The mighty God, The everlasting Father, The Prince of Peace. Of the increase of his government and peace there shall be no end, upon the throne of David, and upon his kingdom, to order it, and to establish it with judgment and with justice from henceforth even for ever."—Isaiah ix. 6, 7.

It is now more than three thousand years ago that God made to Abraham the promise, "In thy seed shall all the nations of the earth be blessed." Again the promise was renewed to Moses when he was commanded to tell the Jews, "a prophet shall the Lord your God raise up unto you, like unto me. Hear ye him . . ." In David's Psalms, again, this same strange person was spoken of who was already, and yet who was to come. David calls him the Son of God, the King of kings. Again, in the Prophets, in many strange and mysterious words, is this same being spoken of as a virgin's child—"Behold a virgin shall conceive and bear a son, and his name shall be called Emmanuel, God with us;" and again, "Unto us a child is born, unto us a son is given, and his name shall be called Wonderful, Counsellor, the Mighty God—the Everlasting Father, the Prince of Peace." And again, "There shall come forth a rod out of the stem of Jesse, and a branch shall grow out of his roots. And the spirit of the Lord shall rest upon him,—the spirit of wisdom and understanding, the spirit of knowledge and the fear of the Lord. And with righteousness shall He judge the poor," &c.

And again, "Thou Bethlehem, though thou be little among the princes of Judah, yet out of thee shall come forth He that is to be ruler in Israel, whose goings forth have been from everlasting. And He shall be great unto the ends of the earth."

But time would fail me if I tried to repeat to you half the passages wherein the old Jewish prophets foretold Him who was to come, and in whom all the nations of the earth should be blessed, more and more clearly as the time drew nigh.

Well, my friends, surely you know of whom I have been speaking—of whom Moses and the prophets spoke—of Him who was born of a village maiden, laid in a manger, proclaimed of angels to the shepherds, worshipped with hymns of glory by the heavenly host on the first Christmas day eighteen hundred and seventy-eight years ago, as we count time. Aye, strange as it may seem, He is come, and in Him all the nations of the earth are blessed. He is come—the Conqueror of Evil—the desire of all nations—the Law-giver—the Lamb which was to suffer for our sins—the King of kings—the Light which should lighten the heathen—the Virgin's child, of wondrous wisdom, whose name should be God as well as man—whom all the heathens, amid strange darkness and mad confusions, had still been fearing and looking for.

He is come—He came on that first Christmas-tide. And we here on each Christmas-tide can thank God for His coming, and say before men and angels, "Unto us a child is born—the Prince of Peace is ours—to His kingdom we belong—He has borne about on Him a man's body, a man's soul and spirit—He was born like us—like us He grew—like us He rejoiced and sorrowed—tempted in all points like as we are, yet without sin—able to the uttermost to understand and help all who come to God by Him. He has bruised the serpent's head—He has delivered us from the power of darkness, and brought us into His kingdom. Through His blood we have redemption and forgiveness—yes! through Him who, though He was laid in a manger, was yet the image of the unseen God. And by Him, and for Him—that Babe of Bethlehem—were all things created in heaven and earth—and He is before all things, and by Him all things consist. All heaven and earth, and all the powers therein, are held together by Him. For it pleased the Father that in Him should all fulness dwell; and having made peace through the blood of His cross, to reconcile by that child all things unto Himself—all things in heaven—all things in earth."

This should be our boast—this should be our glory—for this do we meet together every Christmas day.

But what is all this to us if that Blessed Man be gone away from us? Our souls want more than I have told you yet. Our souls want more than a beautiful and wonderful story about Christ. They want Christ Himself. Preaching is blessed and useful if it speaks of Christ. Our own thoughts are blessed and useful if we think of Christ. The Bible is most blessed and useful containing all things necessary to salvation, for it speaks of Christ. Our prayers are blessed and useful if in them we call and cry earnestly to Christ. But neither preaching, nor thinking, nor praying are enough. In them we think about Him and speak to Him. But we want Him to speak to us. We want not merely a man to say, your sins may be forgiven you; we want Christ Himself to say, "Your sins are forgiven you." We want not merely a wise book to tell us that the good men of old belonged to Christ's kingdom—we want Christ Himself to tell us that we belong to His kingdom. We want not merely a book that tells us that He promised always to be with us—we want Him Himself to tell us that He is really now with us. We want not merely a promise from a prophet of old that in Him all the nations of the earth shall be blessed, but a sign from Christ Himself that this nation of England is really now blest in Him. In short, we want not words, however true words, however fine words, about Christ. We want Christ Himself to forgive us our sins—to give peace and freedom to our hearts—to come to us unseen, and fill us with thoughts and longings such as our fallen nature cannot give us—such thoughts and feelings as we cannot explain in words, for they are too deep and blessed to be talked about—but thoughts which say to us, as if the blessed Jesus Himself spoke to us in the depths of our hearts, "Poor, struggling, sinful brother! thou art mine. For thee I was born—for thee I died—thee I will teach—I will guide thee and inform thee with mine eye—I will never leave thee nor forsake thee."

Well—you want Him—and you want a sign of Him—a sign of His own giving that He is among you this day—a sign of His own giving that He has taken you into His kingdom—a sign of His own giving that He died for you—that He will feed and strengthen your souls in you with His own life and His own body.

Then—there is a sign—there is the sign which has stood stedfast and sure to you—and to your fathers—and your forefathers before them—back for eighteen hundred years, over half the world. There is the bread of which He said, "Take, eat, this is my body which is broken for you." There is the wine of which He said, "This cup is the New Covenant in my blood, which is shed for you, and for many, for the forgiveness of sins." There is His sign. Don't ask how. Don't try to explain it away, and fancy that you can find fitter, and soberer, and safer, and more gospel-sounding words than Jesus Christ's own, by which to speak of His own Sacrament. But say, with the great Queen Elizabeth of old, when men tried too curiously to enquire into her opinion concerning this blessed mystery—

"Christ made the Word and spake it,
He took the bread and brake it,
And what His Word did make it,
That I believe, and take it."

He said, "This bread is my body which was broken for you." He said, "This cup is the New Testament in my blood." Is it? or is it not? And if it is, is not Christ among us now, indeed? Is not that something better than all the preaching in the world? Jesus Christ, the King of kings—the Saviour—the Deliverer—the Lamb of God—the Everlasting Son—the Word—the Light—the Life—is here among us ready to feed our souls in the Holy Sacrament of His body and blood, as surely as that bread and wine will feed our bodies—yea—to feed our souls and bodies to everlasting life. "Ho! every one that thirsteth, come ye to the waters and drink. Come, buy wine without money and without price."

III

IS, OR IS NOT, THE BIBLE TRUE?

"If I say the truth, why do ye not believe Me?"—John viii. 46.

Is, or is not, the Bible true? To this question we must all come some day or other. Do you believe that that book which lies there, which we call the Bible, is a true book, or a lying book? Is it true or false? Is it right or wrong? Is it from God, or is it not from God? Let us answer that. If it is not from God, let it go; but if it is from God, which we know it is, how dare we disobey it?

That God, the maker of heaven and earth, should speak to men—should set His commands down in a book and give it to them—and that they should neglect it, disobey it—it is the strangest sight that can be seen on earth! that God in heaven should say one thing, and a human being, six feet high at most, should dare to do another!

If the Bible is from God, I say, the question is not whether it is better to obey it or not. Better? there is no better or worse in the matter—it is infinitely necessary. To obey is infinitely right, to disobey is infinitely wrong. To obey is infinitely wise, to disobey is infinite folly. There can be no question about the matter, except in the mind of a fool. Better to obey God's word? Better indeed—for to obey is heaven, to disobey is hell. That is the difference. And at your better moments does not the voice within you, witness to, and agree with, the words of that book? When it tells you to care more for your soul than your body—more for the life to come, which is eternity, than for the present life which lasts but a few years—does not common sense tell you that? The Bible tells you to reverence and love God the giver of all good—does not reason tell you that? The Bible tells you loyally to obey, to love, to worship our blessed King and Saviour in heaven. Does not common sense tell you that? Surely if there be such a person as Jesus Christ—if He is sitting now in heaven as Saviour of all, and one day to be Judge of all—by all means He is to be obeyed, He is to be pleased, whoever else we may displease. Reason, one would think, would tell us that—and it is just want of reason which makes us forget it.

What have you to say against the pattern of a true and holy man as laid down in the Bible? The Bible would have you pure—can you deny that you ought to be that? It would have you peaceable—can you deny that you ought to be that? The Bible would have you forgiving, honest, honourable, active, industrious. The Bible would have you generous, loving, charitable. Can you deny that that is right, however some of you may dislike it? The Bible would have you ask all you want from God, and ask forgiveness of God for every offence, great and small, against Him. Can you deny that that is right and reasonable? The Bible would have you live in continual remembrance that the great eye of God is on you—in continual thankfulness to the blessed Saviour who died for you and has redeemed you by His own blood—with daily and hourly prayer for God's Spirit to set your heart and your understanding right on every point. Can you deny that that is all right and good and proper—that unless the Bible be all a dream, and there be no Holy and Almighty God, no merciful Christ in heaven, this is the way and the only way to live? Ay, if there were no God, no Christ, no hereafter, it would be better for man to live as the Bible tells him, than to live as too many do. There would be infinitely less misery, less heart-burnings, less suffering of body and soul, if men followed Christ's example as told us in the Bible. Even if this life were all, and there were neither punishment nor reward for us after death—does not our reason tell us that if all men and women were like Christ in gentleness, wisdom, and purity, the world as long as it lasted would be a heaven?

And do not your own hearts echo these thoughts at moments when they are quietest and purest and most happy too? Have you not said to yourselves—"Those Bible words are good words. After all, if I were like that, I should be happier than I am now." Ah! my friends, listen to those thoughts when they come into your hearts—they are not your own thoughts—they are the voice of One holier than you—wiser than you—One who loves you better than you love yourselves—One pleading with you, stirring you up by His Spirit, if it be but for a moment, to see the things which belong to your peace.

But what can you say for yourselves, if having once had these thoughts, having once settled in your own minds that the Gospel of God is right and you are wrong, if you persist in disobeying that gospel—if you agree one minute with the inner voice, which says, "Do this and live, do this and be at peace with God and man, and your own conscience"—and then fall back the next moment into the same worldly, selfish, peevish, sense-bound, miserable life-in-death as ever?

The reason, my friends, I am afraid, with most of us is, sheer folly—not want of cunning and cleverness, but want of heart—want of feeling—what Solomon calls folly (Prov. i. 22-27), stupidity of soul, when he calls on the simple souls, How long ye simple ones will you love simplicity or silliness, and the scorners delight in their scorning (delight in laughing at what is good), and fools hate knowledge—hate to think earnestly or steadily about anything—the stupidity of the ass, who is too stubborn and thick-skinned to turn out of his way for any one—or the stupidity of the swine, who cares for his food and nothing further—or worse than all, the stupidity of the ape, who cares for nothing but play and curiosity, and the vain and frivolous amusements of the moment.

All these tempers are common enough, and they may be joined with cleverness enough. What beast so clever as an ape? yet what beast so foolish, so mean, so useless? But this is the fault of stupidity—it blinds our eyes to the world of spirits; it makes us forget God; it makes us see first what we can lay our hands on, and nothing more; it makes us forget that we have souls. Our glorious minds and thoughts, which should be stretching on through all eternity, are cramped down to thinking of nothing further than this little hour of earthly life. Our glorious hearts, which should be delighting in everything which is lovely, and generous, and pure, and beautiful, and God-like—ay, delighting in God Himself—are turned in upon themselves, and set upon our own gain, our own ease, our own credit. In short, our immortal souls, made in God's image, become no use to us by this stupidity—they seem for mere salt to keep our bodies from decaying.

Whose work is that? The devil's. But whose fault is it? Do you suppose that the devil has any right in you, any power in you, who have been washed in the waters of baptism and redeemed by Christ from the service of the devil, and signed with His Cross on your foreheads, unless you give him power? Not he. Men's sins open the door to the devil, and when he is in, he will soon trample down the good seed that is springing up, and stamp the mellow soil as hard as iron, so that nothing but his own seeds can grow there, and so keep off the dews of God's spirit, and the working of God's own gospel from making any impression on that hardened stupified soil.

Alas! poor soul. And thy misery is double, because thou knowest not that thou art miserable; and thy misery is treble, because thou hast brought it on thyself!

My friends—there is an ancient fable of the Jews, which, though it is not true, yet has a deep and holy meaning, and teaches an awful lesson.

There lived, says an ancient Jewish Scribe, by the shores of the Dead Sea, a certain tribe of men, utterly given up to pleasure and covetousness, the lust of the flesh, the lust of the eye, and the pride of life. To them the prophet Moses was sent, and preached to them, warning them of repentance and of judgment to come—trying to awaken their souls to high and holy thoughts, and bring them back to the thought of God and heaven. And they, poor fools, listened to Him, admired his preaching, agreed that it all sounded very good—but that he went too far—that it was too difficult—that their present way of life was very pleasant—that they saw no such great need of change, and so on, one excuse after another, till they began to be tired of Moses, and gave him to understand that he was impertinent, troublesome—that they could see nothing wise in him—nothing great; how could they? So Moses went his way, and left them to go theirs. And long after, when some travellers came by, says the fable, they found these foolish people were all changed into dumb beasts; what they had tried to be, now they really were. They had made no use of their souls, and now they had lost them; they had given themselves up to folly, and now folly had taken to her own; they had fancied, as people do every day, that this world is a great play-ground, wherein every one has to amuse himself as he likes best, or at all events a great shop and gambling-house, where the most cunning wins most of his neighbour's money; and now according to their faith it was to them. They had forgotten God and spiritual things, and now they were hid from their eyes. And these travellers found them sitting, playing antics, quarrelling for the fruits of the field—mere beasts—reaping as they had sown, and filled full with the fruit of their own devices.

Only every Sabbath day, says the fable, there came over these poor wretches an awful sense of a piercing Eye watching them from above—a dim feeling that they had been something better and nobler once—a faint recollection of heavenly things which they once knew when they were little children—a blind dread of some awful unseen ruin, into which their miserable empty beast-life was swiftly and steadily sweeping them down;—and then they tried to think and could not—and tried to remember and could not—and so they sat there every Sabbath day, cowering with fear, uneasy and moaning, and half-remembered that they once had souls!

My friends, my friends, are there not too many now-a-days like these poor dwellers by the Dead Sea, who seem to have lost all of God's image except their bodies? who all the week dote on the business and the pleasures of this life, going on very comfortably till they seem to have quite hardened their own souls; and now and then on Sabbath days when they come to church, and pretend to pray and worship, sit all vacant, stupid, their hearts far away, or with a sort of passing uneasiness and dim feeling that all is not right—try to think and cannot—try to pray and cannot—and, like those dwellers by the Dead Sea, once a week on Sabbath day half remember that they once had souls?

So true it is, that from him that hath not, shall be taken away even that which he seemeth to have. So true it is, that the wages of sin is death; death to the soul even in this life. So true it is that why men do not believe Christ, is because they cannot hear His word. So true it is, that only the pure in heart shall see God, or love god-like men and god-like words. So true it is, that he that soweth the wind shall reap the whirlwind, and that he who will not hear Christ's words, shall soon not be able to hear them; that he who will not have Christ for his master, must soon be content to have the devil for his master, and for his wages, spiritual death. From which sad fate of spiritual death may the blessed Saviour, in His infinite mercy, deliver us.

IV

THE TREE OF KNOWLEDGE AND THE TREE OF LIFE

OR

THE FALL

"Now the serpent was more subtile than any beast of the field which the Lord God had made. And he said unto the woman, Yea, hath God said, Ye shall not eat of every tree of the garden? And the woman said unto the serpent, We may eat of the fruit of the trees of the garden: but of the fruit of the tree which is in the midst of the garden, God hath said, Ye shall not eat of it, neither shall ye touch it, lest ye die. And the serpent said unto the woman, Ye shall not surely die. For God doth know that in the day ye eat thereof, then your eyes shall be opened, and ye shall be as gods, knowing good and evil. And when the woman saw that the tree was good for food, and that it was pleasant to the eyes, and a tree to be desired to make one wise, she took of the fruit thereof, and did eat, and gave also unto her husband with her; and he did eat."—
Genesis iii. 1-6.

Here is a lesson for us all. You and I, and all men brought into the world with us a nature which fell in Adam; and, as it fell before we were born, it is certain enough to fall, again and again, after we are born, in this life; ay, and unless we take care, to fall lower and lower, every day, acting Adam's sin over again, until we surely die. This is what I mean—What God said to Adam and Eve, He says to every one of us. And what the devil said to Adam and Eve, he will say to every one of us.

First. God says to us, "Of all the trees of the garden thou mayest freely eat: but of the tree of knowledge of good and evil thou shalt not eat, lest thou die."

Of all the trees of the garden thou mayest freely eat. God grudges you nothing good for you. He has put you into this good and pleasant world, where you will find pleasures enough, and comforts enough, to satisfy you, if you are wise; but there are things which God has forbidden you, not out of any spite or arbitrariness, but because they are bad for you; because they will hurt you if you indulge in them, and sooner or later, kill both body and soul.

Now, many of those wrong things look pleasant enough, and reasonable enough, as the forbidden fruit did. Pleasant to the eyes and good for food—and to be desired to make you wise. As people grow up and go out into life, they are tempted to do many things which their parents forbid, which the Bible forbids, which the law of the land forbids, and they do not understand at first why they are forbidden any more than Adam and Eve understood why they were not to eat of the forbidden fruit.

Then the devil (who is always trying to slander God to us) whispers to them, as he did to Eve, "How unreasonable! how hard on you. People say that this is wrong, and you must not do it, and yet how pleasant it must be! How much money you might get by it—how much wiser, and cleverer, and more able to help yourself you would become, if you went your own way, and did what you like. Surely God is hard on you, and grudges you pleasure. Never mind—don't be afraid. Surely you can judge best what is good for you. Surely you know your own business best. Use your own common sense and do what you like, and what you think will profit you. Are you to be a slave to old rules which your parents or the clergyman taught you?"

So says the devil to every young man as he goes out in life. And to many, alas!—to many, the devil's words sound reasonable enough; they flatter our fallen nature, they flatter our pride and our self-will, and make us fancy we are going up hill, and becoming very fine and manly, and independent and knowing. "Knowing"! How many a young man have I seen run into sin just that he might be knowing; and say, "Why should I not see life for myself? Why should I not know the world, and try what is good, and how I like that, and what is bad too, and how I like that—and then choose for myself like a man, instead of being kept in like a baby?"

So he says exactly what Adam and Eve said in their hearts—"I will eat of the tree of knowledge of good and evil." He says in his heart, too, just what Solomon the wise said, when he, too, determined to eat of the fruit of the tree of knowledge.

Ay, young people, who love to see the world, and to choose for yourselves, read that Book of Ecclesiastes, the saddest book on earth, and get a golden lesson in every verse of it. See how Solomon determined to see life, from the top to the bottom of it. How he "gave his heart to know, seek, and search out by wisdom concerning all things that are done under heaven. I have seen all the works that are done under the sun, and behold, all is vanity and vexation of spirit," (Eccles. i. 13).

And then, how he turned round and gave his heart to know mirth, and madness, and folly, and see whether that was good for him, and, "I said of laughter, it is mad: and of mirth, what doeth it?" (Eccles. ii. 2-26). And then he gave himself to wine and revelling, and after that to riches, and pomp, and glory, and music, and the "fine arts," as we call them. "I made me great works; I builded me houses; I planted me vineyards: I made me gardens and orchards, and I planted trees in them of all kind of fruits: I made me pools of water, to water therewith the wood that bringeth forth trees: I got me servants and maidens, and had servants born in my house; also I had great possessions of great and small cattle above all that were in Jerusalem before me: I gathered me also silver and gold, and the peculiar treasure of kings and of the provinces: I gat me men singers and women singers, and the delights of the sons of men, as musical instruments, and that of all sorts. So I was great, and increased more than all that were before me in Jerusalem: also my wisdom remained with me." And what was the end? "Then I looked on all the works that my hand had done, and on the labour that I had laboured to do: and behold all was vanity and vexation of spirit, and there was no profit under the sun." Therefore, he says, that he hated all the labour he had taken under the sun, because he must leave it to the men who came after him, and found out at last, after years of labour and sorrow, trying to make himself happy with this and that, and finding no rest with any of them, that the conclusion of the whole matter was to "Fear God and keep his commandments, for this is the whole duty of man. For God shall bring every work into judgment, with every secret thing, whether it be good or evil" (Eccles. xii. 13).

So said Solomon—and God knows, my dear friends, God knows, he said truly. Ay, and I know it to be true; and I entreat you this day, in God's name, to hear the conclusion of the whole matter. All this you will find out by eating of the tree of knowledge, and "seeing life," and going your own way, and falling into sin, and smarting for it, for weary years, in anxiety and perplexity, and shame, and sorrow of heart.

All that you will find out thereby—all that Solomon found out thereby,—is just what you know already, and nothing more—just what you have been taught ever since you could speak. "Fear God and keep his commandments, for this is the whole duty of man." Why buy your own experience dear, when you can get it gratis, for nothing already?

Yes; a simple, godly, industrious life, doing the duty which lies nearest you, avoiding sin as you would an adder, because it is sure sooner or later to sting you, if you touch it, is the straight road, and the only road, to happiness, either in this life, or in the life to come. Pleasure and amusement, drinking and jollity, will not make you happy. Money will not make you happy. Cleverness, and cunning, and knowledge of the world will not make you happy. Scholarship and learning will not. But plain, simple righteousness, simply doing right, will.

Do right then and be happy. Obey God's commandments, and you will find that His commandments are Life, and in the pathway thereof there is no death.

Make up your minds to do right, to be right, to keep right by the help of God's Right and Holy Spirit, in the right road. Make up your minds whether you will go through the world in God's way, or your own way—whether you will taste what God has forbidden, and so destroy yourselves, or obey Him and live with Him in bliss. The longer you delay, the more difficult you will find it. Make up your minds now, and ask God to teach you His own heavenly wisdom which is a Tree of Life to all that lay hold on it.

V

I AM

"I AM hath sent me into you."—Exodus iii. 10.

Every day I find it more and more true, that the Bible is full of good news from beginning to end. The Gospel—that is good news—and the best of all good news, is to be found in every book of it; perhaps if we knew how to search the Scriptures, in every chapter and verse of it, from beginning to end. For from beginning to end, from Genesis to Malachi—from the Gospel of St. Matthew to the end of the Revelation—what our Lord said of the Bible stands true: "They (the Scriptures) are they which testify of ME" (John v. 39). The whole Bible testifies, bears witness of Him, the One Unchangeable Christ, who said to Moses, "Say unto the people, I AM hath sent me unto you."

Now let us think a while what that text means; for it has not to do with Moses only, but with all God's prophets, evangelists, preachers. David might have said the same to the Jews in his time, "I AM hath sent me unto you." Elijah, Isaiah, St. Matthew, St. John, St. Paul, might have said the same. And so may God's ministers now. And I, however sinful, or ignorant, or unfaithful to my duty I may be, have still a right to say, as I do now say solemnly and earnestly to you, "I AM hath sent me unto you" this day.

But what do I mean by that? That ought to depend on what Moses meant by it. Moses meant what God meant, and unless I mean the same thing I must mean something wrong. And this is what I think it does mean:

First. I AM—the Lord Jesus Christ told Moses that his name was I AM. Now you perhaps think that this is but a very common place name, for every one can say of himself—I am—and it may seem strange that God should have chosen for His own especial name, words which you and I might have chosen for ourselves just as well. I daresay you think that you may fairly say "you are," and that I can say fairly that "I am."

And yet it is not so. If I say "I am," I say what is not true of me. I must say "I am something—I am a man, I am bad, or I am good, or I am an Englishman, I am a soldier, I am a sailor, I am a clergyman"—and then I shall say what is true of me. But God alone can say "I AM" without saying anything more.

And why? Because God alone is. Everybody and everything else in the world becomes: but God is. We are all becoming something from our birth to our death—changing continually and becoming something different from what we were a minute before; first of all we were created and made, and so became men; and since that we have been every moment changing, becoming older, becoming wiser, or alas! foolisher; becoming stronger or weaker; becoming better or worse. Even our bodies are changing and becoming different day by day.

But God never changes or becomes anything different from what He is now. What He is, that He was, and ever will be. God does not even become older. This may seem very strange, but it is true: for God made Time, God made the years; and once there were no years to count by, no years at all. Remember how long had God Himself been, before He made Time, when there was no Time to pass over? Remember always that God must have created Time. If God did not create Time, no one else did; for there is, as the Athanasian Creed says, "One uncreated and One eternal," even God who made Time as well as all things else.

Am I puzzling you? What I want to do is to make you understand that God's life is quite utterly different from our life, or any way of living and being which we can fancy or think of; lest you make to yourselves the likeness of anything in heaven above or of the earth beneath, and think that God is like that and so worship it, and have other gods beside the true God, and so break the first and second commandments, as thousands do who fancy themselves good Protestants, and hate Popery and idolatry, and yet worship a very different sort of god from the "I AM," who sent Moses to the children of Israel. Remember then this at least, that God was before all things, and all worlds, and all Time; so that there was a time when there were no worlds, and a time when there was no Time—nothing but God alone, absolute, eternal, neither made nor created, the same that He is now and will be for ever.

When I say "God is," that is a very different thing from God Himself saying, "I AM." A different thing? Oh! my friends, here is the root of the whole Gospel, the root of all our hope for this world and for the world to come—for ourselves, for our own future, and the future of all the world. Do you not see how? Then I will try to explain.

Many heathen men have known that there was one eternal God, and that God is. But they did not know that God Himself had said so; and that made them anxious, puzzled, almost desperate, so that the wiser they were, the unhappier they were. For what use is it merely knowing that "God is"? The question for poor human creatures is, "But what sort of a being is God? Is He far off? Millions of miles from this earth? Does He care nothing about us? Does He let the world go its own way right or wrong? Is He proud and careless? A self-glorifying Deity whose mercy is not over all His works, or even over any of them? Or does He care for us? Does He see us? Will He speak to us? Has He ever spoken to any one? Has He ever told any one about Himself?" There is the question—the question of all questions. And if a man once begins thinking about his own soul, and this world, and God,—till he gets that question answered, he can have no comfort about himself or the world, or anything—till in fact he knows whether God has ever spoken to men or not.

And the glory of the Bible, the power of God revealed in the Bible, is, that it answers the question, and says, "God does care for men, God does see men, God is not far off from any one of us." Ay, God speaks to men—God spoke to Moses and said, not "God is" but "I AM." God in sundry times and in divers manners spoke to our fathers by the Prophets and said "I AM."

But more—Moses said, "I AM hath sent me." God does not merely love us, and yet leave us to ourselves. He sends after us. He sends to us. In old times He sent prophets and wise men one after the other to preach repentance and righteousness, and to teach men all that was good for them; and when men would not listen to them, but shut their ears to them and drove them out, killing some and beating some, God was so determined to send to men, so unwearied, so patient, so earnest, so loving still, that He said, "I will send now my own Son, surely they will hear Him."

Yes, my friends, this is the I AM. This is God—this is our God—this is our Heavenly Father; not a proud and selfish Being, who looks down haughtily from afar off on all the misery and ignorance of the world, but as a wise man of old said, "A most merciful God, a revealer of secrets, who showeth to man the things which he knew not." This is our God—not a tyrant, but a Deliverer—not a condemning God, but a saving God, who wills that none should perish, who sends to seek and to save those who are lost, who sends His sun to shine on the just and the unjust, and is good to the unthankful and the evil. A God who so loved the world which He had made, in spite of all its sin and follies, that He spared not His only begotten Son, but freely gave Him for it. A God who sits on His throne for ever judging right, and ministering true judgment among the people, who from His throne beholds all those who dwell upon the earth, and fashions the hearts of them, and understandeth all their works. A God who comes out of His place to visit the wrong done on the earth, and be a refuge for the oppressed, and a help in time of trouble, to help the fatherless and poor unto their right, that the men of this world be no more exalted against them.

This is our God. This is our Father—always condescending, always patient, always loving, always just. And always active, always working to do good to all his creatures, like that exact pattern and copy of Himself, the Lord Jesus Christ, who said, "My Father worketh hitherto, and I work." (John v. 17).

But again: "I AM hath sent me unto you."

Unto whom? Who was Moses sent to? To the Children of Israel in Egypt. And what sort of people were they? Were they wise and learned? On the contrary they were stupid, ignorant, and brutish. Were they pious and godly? On the contrary they were worshipping the foolish idols of the Egyptians—so fond of idolatry that they must needs make a golden calf and worship it. Were they respectable and cleanly livers? Were they teachable and obedient? On the contrary, they were profligate, stiff-necked, murmurers, disobedient, unwilling to trust God's goodness, though He had shown them all those glorious signs and wonders for their sakes, and brought them out of Egypt with a mighty hand and a stretched-out arm. Were they high-spirited and brave? On the contrary, they were mean-spirited and cowards, murmuring against Moses and against God, if anything went wrong, for setting them free; ready to go back and be slaves to the Egyptians rather than face danger and fight; looking back and longing after the flesh-pots of Egypt, where they eat bread to the full, and willing to be slaves again and have all their men children drowned in the river, and themselves put to hard labour in the brick kilns, if they could only fill their stomachs. And even at best when Moses had brought them to the very edge of that rich land of Canaan, which God had promised them, they were afraid to go into it, and win it for themselves; and God had to send them back again, to wander forty years in the wilderness, till all that cowardly, base, first generation, who came up out of Egypt was dead, and a new generation had grown up, made brave and hardy by their long training in the deserts, and taught to trust and obey God from their youth; and so able and willing to conquer the good land which God had promised them.

Altogether the Children of Israel, to whom God sent Moses, were plainly an ignorant, brutish, cowardly set of people, fallen lower far than the negroes of South America, fit to be slaves and nothing better.

Then why did God take such trouble for them? Why did God care for them, and help them, and work wonders for them? Why?

Exactly because they were so bad. He that hath ears to hear let him hear, and understand by this example of all examples what manner of God our God is. Just because they were so bad, His goodness yearned over them all the more, and longed to make them good. Just because they were so unclean and brutish His holiness longed all the more to cleanse them. Because they were so stupid and ignorant, His wisdom longed to make them wise. Because they were so miserable, His pity yearned over them, as a father over a child fallen into danger. Because they were sick, they had all the more need of a physician. Because they were lost, there was all the more reason for seeking and saving them. Because they were utterly weak, God desired all the more to put His strength into them, that His strength might be made perfect in weakness.

True, God's goodness seemed of little use to too many of them. Their history during the next forty years was a very sad one. With many of them God was not well pleased, the Bible tells us, and their carcases fell in the Wilderness. A sad forty years they were for Moses also, as he says in that sad and glorious Psalm of his (Ps. xc. 7, 8): "We consume away in thy displeasure, and are afraid of thy wrathful indignation. Thou hast set our misdeeds before us, our secret sins in the light of thy countenance, for when Thou art angry our days are gone: we bring our years to an end as a tale that is told."

But that was all their own fault. God never left them for all those forty years. He fed them with manna in the wilderness, and the angel of His presence preserved them.

And now, my friends, remember what I have said of God in this text, "I AM hath sent me unto you," and see how it preaches to you an almighty, unchangeable Father, whose mercy is over all His works, full of love and care for all, longing and labouring for ever by His Son Jesus Christ to raise us from the death of sin (which is the only death we need to be afraid of) to the life of righteousness—the only life worth living here, the only life which we can live beyond the grave! A just God, a merciful God, a patient God, a generous God, a gracious God; a God whose glory is to save—a God who is utterly worthy of our love and respect—a God whom we can trust—a God whom it is worth while to obey—a God who deserves our thanks from our cradle to our grave—a God to whom we ought honestly, and from the bottom of our hearts to say, now and for ever:

"We worship Thee, we bless Thee, we praise Thee, we magnify Thee, we give thanks to Thee for Thy great glory, oh! Lord God, Heavenly King, God the Father Almighty."

VI

THE ENGLISHMAN TRAINED BY TOIL

"All the commandments which I command thee this day shall ye observe to do, that ye may live, and multiply, and go in and possess the land which the Lord sware unto your fathers. And thou shalt remember all the way which the Lord thy God led thee these forty years in the wilderness, to humble thee, and to prove thee, to know what was in thine heart, whether thou wouldest keep his commandments, or no. And he humbled thee, and suffered thee to hunger, and fed thee with manna, which thou knewest not, neither did thy fathers know; that he might make thee know that man doth not live by bread only, but by every word that proceedeth out of the mouth of the Lord doth man live.... Thou shall also consider in thine heart that, as a man chasteneth his son, so the Lord thy God chasteneth thee."—Deut. viii. 1, 2, 3, 5.

As God led the Jews through the wilderness, so He leads us through the journey of life. As God called on the Jews to rejoice in Him, and to bless Him for going with them, and teaching and training them by dangers and sorrows; so He calls on us to lift up our hearts and bless Him for teaching and training us in the battle of life.

But some of you may say, "Why do you ask us to thank God for lessons which we have bought by labour and sorrow? Are not our sorrows more than our joys? Our labour far heavier than our rest can be sweet? You tell us to be joyful and thank God for His mercies; but why all this toil? Why must we work on, and on, and on, all our days, in weariness and anxiety? Why must we only toil, toil, till we die, and lie down, fairly conquered and worn out, on that stern mother earth, from whom we have been wringing our paltry livelihood from our boyhood to our grave? What is our life but labour and sorrow?"

Are not some of you thinking in this way to-day? Have I not guessed the hearts of some of you at least? And is not this a strange way of making you joyful to remind you of these thoughts?

My friends, be sure I only remind you of these sad thoughts, because they are true thoughts, because God meant you to bear them and face them like men; because you must have these thoughts, and let them make you sad, and make up your minds to face them again and again, before even you can thank God really like redeemed, immortal Christian men and women. And believe me, I would not mention these sad thoughts, if I had not a remedy for them. If I had not a message to you from the living God, and Christ the King of the earth, whereby I tell you now to rejoice and give thanks to Him in spite of all your labour and sorrow. Ay more, I say, Rejoice and give thanks on account of all your labour and sorrow, and count it all joy when ye fall into divers tribulations.

It is true, my friends, we are a hard working and a somewhat sad race of men, we English. The life of the working man is labour and sorrow, and so is the life of the scholar, and so is the life of even many a rich man. All things are full of labour in England. Man cannot utter it, the eye is not satisfied with seeing, nor the ear with hearing; we are the wisest of all nations; and yet as Solomon says, behold in much wisdom is much grief; and in increasing knowledge, we still increase sorrow.

Truly, I may say of us Englishmen, as Paul said of the Christians of his time, that if Christ be not raised from the dead, and if in this life only we have hope in Him, we are of all nations one of the most unhappy. When we look at all the hundreds of thousands pent up in our great cities among filth and smoke, toiling in factories, in workshops, in dark mines under ground—when we think of the soldier on the march under the sultry sun of India, the sailor on the stormy sea—when we think of this our bleak inclement climate, our five months of winter every year;—no man's food and clothing to be gained but by bitter toil, either of himself or of others—and then when we compare our lot with that of the dwellers in hot countries, in India and in Africa, and the islands of the South Seas, where men live with no care, no labour—where clothes and fire are never needed—where every tree bears delicious food, and man lives in perpetual summer, in careless health and beauty, among continual mirth and ease, like the birds which know no care—then it seems at moments as if God had been unfair in giving so much more to the savage than He has to us, of the blessings of this earthly life; and we are led to long that our lot was cast in those fruitful and delicious climates of the South, in a continual paradise of mirth and plenty, and beauty and sunshine.

But no, my friends, we are more blest than the careless Indian who never knows what labour is; his life is but the life of the butterfly, which flutters from flower to flower and sports in the sunshine, and sucks sweets for a brief hour, and then perishes without hope. His life is a dream, he sees no heaven before him, he knows no glorious God, with the sight of whom he is to be blest for ever. His body may be in perpetual ease, and health, and beauty for a few short years, but what care has he for his undying spirit, that is blind and dead within him?

But to bring a man's soul to life, to train and educate a man's soul that it may go on from strength to strength, and glory to glory till it appears in the presence of God—that wants a stern and a severe training of sorrow and labour, of which the poor, pampered, luxurious savage knows nothing. This is why Christ brought our forefathers into this bleak, cold, northern land, and forced them to gain their bread by the sweat of their brows, and the sorrows of their hearts, and to keep their land by many wars.

Now this is the reason of our carefulness, of our many troubles, that God is educating and training us English; that He will not have us be savages, but Christian citizens; He will have us not merely happy, but blessed through all eternity. He will not have us to be like the poor Indians, slaves to our flesh and our appetites—slaves to the pleasant things around us; but He will have us fill the earth and subdue it; He will have England the light of the nations—and Englishmen preach freedom, and wisdom, and prudence, and the gospel of Jesus Christ to all the nations of the earth. Therefore Christ afflicts us because He loves us, because whom He loveth He chasteneth, and scourgeth every son whom He receiveth. Because He has ordained England to preach the Cross, therefore He will have England bear the cross.

It has often struck me, my friends, as a beautiful and a deep sign, a blessed ordinance of the great and wise God, that the flag of England, and especially the flag of our navy—the flag which is loved and reverenced through all the world, as the bringer of free communion between nation and nation, the bringer of order and equal justice and holy freedom, and the divine majesty of law, and the light of the blessed gospel wherever it goes; that this flag, I say, should be the red-cross flag, the flag of the Cross of Christ—a double sign—a sign to all men that we are a Christian nation, a gospel people; and a sign, too, to ourselves, that we are meant to bear Christ's cross—to bear the afflictions which He lays upon us—to be made perfect through sufferings, to crucify the flesh with its affections and lusts, that we may be brave and self-denying; going forth in Christ's strength, remembering that it is He who gives us power to get wealth; that we ought to fight His battles, that we ought to spread His name at home and abroad; and rejoice in every sorrow, which teaches us more and more the blessed meaning of His saving name, and the share which we have in it.

I have said that we are a melancholy people. Foreigners all say of us, that we are the saddest of all people; that when they come to England, they are struck with our silence, and gloominess, and careworn faces, and our want of merriment and cheerfulness. And yet, with all this, we are the greatest of nations at this day—the strongest and the most industrious and the wisest. The gospel of Jesus Christ is preached oftener, and more simply, and more fully here in England than in any nation, and I dare to say it, that in spite of all our sins, there are as many or more of God's true saints, more holy men and women among English people at this moment, than among any people of the earth. And why? because there are so many among us who have hope in Christ beyond this life, who look for everlasting salvation through all eternity to His name. If in this life only we have hope in Christ, truly of all people we should be most miserable; but Christ is risen from the dead, and He has ascended up on high, and led captivity captive, and received gifts for men. He sits even now at God's right hand praying for us. To Him all power is given in heaven and earth, and He is our covenant God and Saviour, He is our King. He is ours; and He will have us put on His likeness, and with Him be made perfect through sufferings—through sufferings, for sorrow is the gate of life. Through much tribulation we enter into the kingdom of God; without weary pain none of us is born into the world; without weary labour not a harvest in England is grown and reaped; without weary thought, and teaching, and correction, not a child among us is educated to be a man; without weary thought and weary labour, not one of us can do his duty in that station of life to which Christ has called him. Not without weary struggles and arguings and contentions, by martyrdoms, by desperate wars, our forefathers won for us our religion, our freedom and our laws, which make England the wonder of the world. This is the great law of our life—to be made perfect through sufferings, as our Lord and Master was before us. He has dealt with us, as my text tells you He dealt with the Jews, His chosen people of old, as He deals with every soul of man on whom He sets His love. "All the commandments which I command thee this day shall ye observe to do, that ye may live, and multiply, and go in and possess the land which the Lord sware unto your fathers. And thou shalt remember all the way which the Lord thy God led thee these forty years in the wilderness, to humble thee, and to prove thee, to know what was in thine heart, whether thou wouldest keep His commandments, or no. And He humbled thee, and suffered thee to hunger, and fed thee with manna, which thou knewest not, neither did thy fathers know; that He might make thee know that man doth not live by bread only, but by every word that proceedeth out of the mouth of the Lord doth man live . . . Thou shalt also consider in thine heart, that, as a man chasteneth his son, so the Lord thy God chasteneth thee."

For, believe me, my friends, whatever nation or whatever man Christ chooses to be His own, and to be holy and noble and glorious with Him, He makes them perfect through suffering. First, He stirs up in them strange longings after what is great and good. He makes them hunger and thirst after righteousness, and then He lets them see how nothing on this earth, nothing beautiful or nothing pleasant which they can get or invent for themselves will satisfy; and so He teaches them to look to Him, to look for peace and salvation from heaven and not from earth. Then He leads them, as He led the Jews of old, through the wilderness and through the sea, through strange afflictions, through poverty, and war, and labour, that they may learn to know that He is leading them and not themselves; that they may learn to trust not in themselves, but in Him; not in their own strength: but in the bread which cometh down from heaven; not in their own courage, but in Him; and just when all seems most hopeless, He makes one of them chase a thousand, and by strange and unexpected providences, and the courage which a just cause inspires, brings His people triumphant through temptation and danger, and puts to flight the armies of the heathen, and the inventions of the evil fiend, and glorifies His name in His chosen people.

So He calls out in the heart of men and of the heart of nations, the two great twin virtues, which always go hand in hand—Faith in God, and Faith in themselves. He lets them feel themselves foolish that they may learn how to be wise in His wisdom. He lets them find themselves weak that they may learn how to be strong in His strength. Then sometimes He lets them follow their own devices and be filled with the fruits of their own inventions. He lets their sinful hearts have free course down into the depths of idolatry and covetousness, and filthy pleasure and mad self-conceit, that they may learn to know the bitter fruit that springs from the accursed root of sin, and come back to Him in shame and repentance, entreating Him to inform their thoughts, and guide their wills, and gather them to Him as a hen gathereth her chickens under her wing, that they may never more wander from Him, their life, their light, and their Saviour. Then, sometimes, if His children forsake His laws and break His covenant, He visits their offences with the rod, and their sin with the stripes of the children of men. That is, He punishes them as He punishes the heathen, if they sin as the heathen sin. He lets loose upon them His wrath, war, disease, or scarcity, that He may drive them back to Him.

And all the while He will have them labour. He will make them try their strength, and use their strength, and improve their strength of soul and body. By making them labour, Christ teaches His people industry, order, self-command, self-denial, patience, courage, endurance, foresight, thoughtfulness, earnestness. All these blessed virtues come out of holy labour; by working in welldoing we learn lessons which the savage among his delicious fruits and flowers, in his life of golden ease, and luxurious laziness, can never learn.

And all this Christ teaches us because He loves us, because He would have us perfect. His love is unchangeable. As He swore by Himself that He would never fail David, so He has sworn that He will never fail any one of His Churches, or any one of us. Lo, said He, I am with you always, even to the end of the world. Nothing shall separate us from the love of Christ; neither battle nor famine, nor anything else in heaven or earth. All He wants is to educate us, because He loves us. He doth not afflict willingly nor grieve the children of men. And because He is a God of love, He proves His love to us every now and then by blessing us, as well as by correcting us; else our spirits would fail before Him, and the souls which He has made. When He sees our adversity, He hears our complaint, He thinks upon His covenant and pities us, according to the multitude of His mercies. "A fruitful land maketh He barren for the wickedness of them that dwell therein, yet when they cry unto the Lord in their trouble, He delivereth them out of their distress. He maketh the wilderness standing water, and water springs of dry ground, and there He setteth the hungry that they may build them a city, that they may sow their lands and plant vineyards, to yield them fruits of increase. He blesseth them, so that they multiply exceedingly, and suffereth not their cattle to decrease; and again, when they are diminished or brought low through affliction, through any plague or trouble, though He suffer them to be evil entreated by tyrants, and let them wander out of the way in the wilderness; yet helpeth He the poor out of misery, and maketh them households like a flock of sheep." (Ps. cvii.)

O my friends, have not these words ever been wonderfully fulfilled to some of you! Then see how true it is that God will not always be chiding, neither keepeth He His anger for ever; but He knoweth our frame, He remembereth that we are but dust, and like as a father pitieth his children, so does He pity those who fear Him; and oftentimes, too, in His great condescension, those who fear Him not.

My friends, I have been trying in this sermon to make you feel that you are under God's guidance, that His providence is trying to train and educate you. I have told you that there is a blessed use and meaning in your very sorrows, and in this life of continual toil which God has appointed for you; I have told you that you ought to thank God for those sorrows: how much more then ought you to thank Him for your joys. If you should thank Him for want, surely you should thank Him for plenty. O thank Him earnestly—not only with your lips, but in your lives. If you believe that He has redeemed you with His precious blood, show your thankfulness by living as redeemed men, holy to God—who are not your own, but bought with a price; therefore show forth God's glory, the power of His grace in your bodies and your spirits which are His. If you feel that it is a noble thing to be an Englishman—especially an English soldier or an English sailor—a noble and honourable privilege to be allowed to do your duty in the noblest nation and the noblest church which the world ever saw—then live as Englishmen in covenant with God; faithful to Him who has redeemed you and washed you from your sins in His own blood. Do you be faithful and obedient to Christ's Spirit, and He will be faithful to those promises of His. Though a thousand fall at thy right hand, yet the evil shall not come nigh thee. Blessed are all they that fear the Lord and walk in His ways. For thou shalt eat the labours of thine hand. O well art thou and happy shalt thou be. The Lord out of heaven shall so bless thee, that thou shalt see England in prosperity all thy life long. Yea, thou shalt see thy children's children, and peace upon thy native land.

Oh, remember how God fulfilled that promise to England seventy years ago, when the French swept in fire and slaughter, and horrors worse than either, over almost every nation in Europe, while England remained safe in peace and plenty, and an enemy never set foot on God's chosen English soil. Remember the French war, and our salvation in it, and then believe and take comfort. Trust in the Lord and be doing good; dwell in the land, and verily thou shalt be fed.

VII

HIGHER OR LOWER: WHICH SHALL WIN?

"Therefore, brethren, we are debtors, not to the flesh, to live after the flesh. For if ye live after the flesh, ye shall die: but if ye through the spirit do mortify the deeds of the body, ye shall live. For as many as are led by the spirit of God, they are the sons of God. For ye have not received the spirit of bondage again to fear; but ye have received the Spirit of adoption, whereby we cry, Abba, Father."—Romans viii. 12-15.

Let us try to understand these words. They are of quite infinite importance to us all.

We shall all agree, all of us at least who have thought at all about right and wrong, and tried to do right and avoid wrong—that there goes on in us, at times, a strange struggle. We wish to do a right thing, and at the very same time long to do a wrong one. We are pulled, as it were, two different ways by two different feelings, feel as if we were two men at once, a better man and a worse man struggling for the mastery. One may conquer, or the other. We may be like the confirmed drunkard who cannot help draining off his liquor, though he knows that it is going to kill him; or we may be like the man who conquers his love for drink, and puts the liquor away, because he knows that he ought not to take it.

We know too well, many of us, how painful this inward struggle is, between our better selves, and our worse selves. How discontented with ourselves it makes us, how ashamed of ourselves, how angry with ourselves. We all understand too well—or ought to understand, St. Paul's words: How often the good which he wished to do, he did not do, but the evil which he did not wish to do, he did. How he delighted in the law of God in his inward man; but he found another law in him, in his body, warring against the law of his mind—that is his conscience and reason, and making a slave of him till he was ready at times to cry, "Oh wretched man that I am, who shall deliver me from the body of this death?"

We can understand too, surely the famous parable of Plato, the greatest of heathen philosophers, who says, that the soul of man is like a chariot, guided by a man's will, but drawn by two horses. The one horse he says is white, beautiful and noble, well-broken and winged, too, always trying to rise and fly upward with the chariot toward heaven. But the other horse is black, evil, and unmanageable, always trying to rush downward, and drag the chariot and the driver into hell.

Ah my friends, that is but too true a picture of most of us, and God grant that in our souls the better horse may win, that our nobler and purer desires may lift us up, and leave behind those lower and fouler desires which try to drag us down. But to drag us down whither? To hell at last, says Plato the heathen. To destruction and death in the meanwhile, says St. Paul.

Now in the text St. Paul explains this struggle—this continual war which goes on within us. He says that there are two parts in us—the flesh and the spirit—and that the flesh lusts, that is, longs and struggles to have its own way against the spirit, and the spirit against the flesh. First, there is a flesh in us—that is, a carnal animal nature. Of that there can be no doubt: we are animals, we come into the world as animals do—eat, drink, sleep as they do—have the same passions as they have—and our carnal mortal bodies die at last, exactly as the animals die.

But are we nothing more? God forbid. St. Paul tells us that we are something more—and our own conscience and reason tell us that we are something more. We know that to be a man, we must be something more than an animal—a mere brute—for when we call any one a brute, what do we mean? That he has lost his humanity, his sense of justice, mercy, and decency, and given himself up to his flesh—his animal nature, till the man in him is dead, and only the brute remains. Mind, I do not say that we are right in calling any human being a brute, for no one, I believe, is sunk so low, but there is some spark of humanity, some spark of what St. Paul calls "the spirit," left in him, which may be fanned into a flame and conquer, and raise and save the man at last—unless he be a mere idiot—or that most unhappy and brutal of all beings, a confirmed drunkard.

But our giving way to the same selfish shameless passions, which we see in the lower animals, is letting the "brute" in us conquer, is giving way to the works of the flesh. The shameless and profligate person gives way to the "brute" within him—the man who beats his wife—or ill-treats his children—or in any wise tyrannises over those who are weaker than himself, he too gives way to the "brute" within him. He who grudges, envies, tries to aggrandise himself at his neighbour's expense—he too gives way to the "brute" within him, and puts on the likeness of the dog which snatches and snarls over his bone. He who spends his life in cunning plots and mean tricks, stealthy, crafty, silent, false, he gives way to the "brute" in him, just as much as the fox or ferret. And those, let me say, who without giving way to those grosser vices, let their minds be swallowed up with vanity, love of admiration, always longing to be seen and looked at, and wondering what folks will say of them, they too give way to the flesh, and lower themselves to the likeness of animals. As vain as a peacock, says the old proverb. And shame it is to any human being so far to forget his true humanity, as to have that said of him. And what shall we say of them who like the swine live only for eating and drinking, and enjoyment? Or what of those who like the butterflies spend all their time in frivolous amusement, fluttering in the sunshine, silly and helpless, without a sense of duty or usefulness, without forethought for the coming frosts of winter, against which their gay feathers would be no protection? Do not all these in some way or other give way to the animal within them, and live after the flesh? And do they not, all of them, of the flesh, reap corruption, and fulfil St. Paul's words, "If ye live after the flesh ye shall die?"

But some one will say—"Die?—of course we shall all die—good and bad alike." Is it so, my friends? Then why does our Lord say, "He that liveth and believeth in me shall never die?" And why does St. Paul say, "If ye through the spirit do mortify," that is crush, and as it were kill, "the deeds of the body," all those low animal passions and vices, "ye shall live."

Let us look at the text again. "If ye live after the flesh ye shall die." If you give way to those animal passions and vices—low and cruel—or even merely selfish and frivolous, you shall die; not merely your bodies—they will die in any case—the animals do—for animals they are, and as animals die they must. But over and above that—you yourselves shall die—your character will die, your manhood or your womanhood will die, your immortal soul will die. The likeness of God in you will die. Oh, my friends, there is a second death to which that first death of the body is a mere trivial and harmless accident—the death of sin which kills the true man and true woman within you. And that second death may begin in this life, and if it be not stopped and cured in time, may go on for ever. The black horse of which I spoke just now, may get the mastery and drag us down, down, into bogs out of which we can never rise—over cliffs which we can never climb again—down lower and lower—more and more foolish, more and more reckless, more and more base, more and more wretched. And then there will be no more use in saying, "The Lord have mercy on my soul," for we shall have no soul left to have mercy on.

This is the dark side of the matter—a very dark one: but it has to be spoken of, because it is true; and what is more, it comes true only too often in this world. God grant, my dear friends, that it may not come true of any of you.

But there is also a bright side to the matter—and on that I will speak now, in order that this sermon may end, as such gospel sermons surely should end, not with threats and fear, but with hope and comfort.

"If ye through the spirit do mortify the deeds of the body, ye shall live." If you will be true to your better selves, if you will listen to, and obey the spirit of God, when He puts into your hearts good desires, and makes you long to be just and true, pure and sober, kind and useful. If you will cast away and trample under foot animal passions, low vices, you shall live. You shall live. Your very soul and self shall live, and live for ever. Your humanity, your human nature shall live. All that is humane in you shall live. All that is merciful and kind in you, all that is pure and graceful, all that is noble and generous, all that is useful. All in you that is pleasant to yourselves shall live. All in you that is pleasant to your neighbours. All in you that is pleasant to God shall live. In one word, all in you that is like Christ—all in you that is like God—all in you that is spirit and not flesh, shall live, and live for ever. So it must be, for what says St. Paul? "As many as are led by the spirit of God, they are the sons of God." Those who let the spirit of God lead them upward instead of letting their own animal nature drag them downward, they are the sons of God. And how can a son of God perish? How can that which is like God and like Christ perish? How can he perish, who like Christ is full of the fruits of the spirit? of love, joy, peace, long-suffering, gentleness, goodness, faith, meekness, temperance? The world did not give them to him, and the world cannot take them from him. They were not bestowed on him at his bodily birth—neither shall they be taken from him at his bodily death—for those blessed fruits of the spirit belong neither to the flesh nor to the world, but to Christ's spirit, and to heaven—to that heaven in which they dwell before the throne of God—yea, rather in the mind of God Himself, the eternal forms of the truth, the beauty, the goodness—which were before all worlds—and shall be after all worlds have passed away.

Oh! choose my friends, especially you who are young and entering into life. Remember the parable of the old heathen, about the two horses who draw your soul. Choose in time whether the better horse shall win, or the worse; whether your better self, or your worse, the Spirit of God or your own flesh, shall be your master—whether you will rise step by step to heaven, or sink step by step to death and hell? And let no one tell you. That is not the question. That is not what we care about. We know we shall do a great many wrong things before we die. Every one does that; but we hope we shall be able to make our peace with God before we die, and so be forgiven at last.

My dear friends, that kind of religion has done more harm than most kinds of irreligion. It tells you to take your chance of beginning at the end—that is just before you die. Common sense tells you that the only way to get to the end, is by beginning at the beginning, which is now. Now is the accepted time. Now is the day of salvation, and you are accepted now, already, long ago.

What do you or any man want with making your peace with God? You are at peace with God already. He has made His peace with you. An infinitely better peace than any priest or preacher can make for you. You are God's child. He looks down on you with boundless love. The great heart of Christ, your King, your Redeemer, your elder brother, yearns over you with boundless longing to draw you up to Him, that you may be noble as He is noble, pure as He is pure, loving as He is loving, just as He is just. Try to be that. God will at the last day take you as He finds you. Let Him find you such as that—walking not after the flesh, but after the Spirit; and then, and then only, there will be no condemnation for you, for you will be in Christ Jesus. Do not—do not talk about making your peace with God some day—like a naughty child playing truant till the last moment, and hoping that the schoolmaster may forget to punish it. No, I trust you have received the Spirit. If you have, then look facts in the face. I trust that none of you have received the Spirit of bondage, which is slavery again unto fear. If you have God's Spirit you will see who you are, and where you are, and act accordingly—you will see that you are God's children, who are meant to be educated by the Son of God, and led by the Spirit of God, and raised day by day, year by year, from the death of sin, to the life of righteousness, from the likeness of the brute animal, to the likeness of Christ, the Son of Man!

VIII

ST. PETER

OR

TRUE COURAGE

"Now when they saw the boldness of Peter and John, and perceived that they were unlearned and ignorant men, they marvelled; and they took knowledge of them, that they had been with Jesus. And they called them, and commanded them not to speak at all nor teach in the name of Jesus. But Peter and John answered and said unto them, Whether it be right in the sight of God to hearken unto you more than unto God, judge ye."— Acts iv 13, 18, 19.

I think that the quality, the grace of God, which St. Peter's character and story specially forces on our notice is courage—the true courage which comes by faith. The courage which comes by faith, I say. There is a courage which does not come by faith. There is a brute courage which comes from hardness of heart; from obstinacy, or anger, or stupidity, which does not see danger, or does not feel pain. That is the courage of the brute. One does not blame it or call it wrong. It is good in its place, as all natural things are which God has made. It is good enough for the brute; but it is not good enough for man. You cannot trust it in man. And the more a man is what a man should be, the less he can trust it. The more mind and understanding a man has, so as to be able to foresee danger and measure it, the more chance there is of his brute courage giving way. The more feeling a man has, the more keen he is to feel pain of body, or pain of mind, such as shame, loneliness, the dislike of ridicule, and the contempt of his fellow-men; in a word, the more of a man he is, the more chance there is of his brute courage breaking down, just when he wants it more to keep him up, and leaving him to play the coward and come to shame.

Yes; to go through with a difficult or dangerous undertaking a man wants more than brute courage. He wants spiritual courage, the courage which comes by faith. He needs to have faith in what he is doing to be certain that he is doing his duty—to be certain that he is in the right. To give one example. Look at the class of men who in all England in times of peace undergo the most fearful dangers; who know not at what hour of any night they may not be called up to the most serious and hard labour and responsibility, with the chance of a horrible and torturing death. I mean the firemen of our great cities, than whom there are no steadier, braver, nobler-hearted men. Not a week passes without one or more of those firemen, in trying to save life and property, doing things which are altogether heroic. What do you fancy keeps them up to their work? High pay? The amusement and excitement of the fires? The vanity of being praised for their courage? My friends, those would be but weak and paltry motives, which would not keep a man's heart calm and his head clear under such responsibility and danger as theirs.

No; it is the sense of duty. The knowledge that they are doing a good and a noble work in saving the lives of human beings and the wealth of the nation—the knowledge that they are in God's hands, and that no evil can happen to him who is doing right—that to him even death at his post is not a loss, but a gain. In short, faith in God, more or less clear, is what gives those men their strong and quiet courage. God grant that you and I, if ever we have dangerous work to do, may get true courage from the same fountain of ghostly strength.

Yes; it is the courage which comes by faith which makes truly brave men, men like St. Peter and St. John, who can say, "If I am right, God is on my side, I will not fear what men can do unto me." "I will not fear," said David, "though the earth be moved, and the mountains carried into the midst of the sea." The just man who holds firm to his duty will not, says a wise old writer, "be shaken from his solid mind by the rage of the mob bidding him do base things, or the frown of the tyrant who persecutes him. Though the world were to crumble to pieces round him, its ruins would strike him without making him tremble."

Such courage has made men, shut up in prison for long weary years for doing what was right, endure manfully for the sake of some great cause, and say—

"Stone walls do not a prison make,
Nor iron bars a cage,
Minds innocent and quiet take
That for an hermitage.
If I have freedom in my thought,

And in my soul am free,
Angels alone that soar above
Enjoy such liberty."

Yes; settle it in your hearts, all of you. There is but one thing you have to fear in heaven or earth—being untrue to your better selves, and therefore untrue to God. If you will not do the thing you know to be right, and say the thing you know to be true, then indeed you are weak. You are a coward, and sin against God. And you will suffer the penalty of your cowardice. You desert God, and therefore you cannot expect Him to stand by you. But who will harm you if you be followers of that which is right?

What does David say:—"Lord, who shall abide in thy tabernacle? who shall dwell in thy holy hill? He that walketh uprightly, and worketh righteousness, and speaketh the truth in his heart. He that backbiteth not with his tongue, nor doeth evil to his neighbour, nor taketh up a reproach against his neighbour. In whose eyes a vile person is contemned; but he honoureth them that fear the Lord. He that sweareth to his own hurt, and changeth not. He that putteth not out his money to usury, nor taketh reward against the innocent. He that doeth these things shall never be moved."—Psalm xv. 1-5. Yes, my friends, there is a tabernacle of God in which, even in this life, He will hide us from strife. There is a hill of God in which, even in the midst of danger, and labour, and anxiety, we may rest both day and night—even Jesus Christ, the Rock of Ages—He who is the righteousness itself, the truth itself. And whosoever does righteousness and speaks truth, dwells in Christ in this life, as well as in the life to come. And Christ will give him courage to strengthen him by His Holy Spirit, to stand in the evil day, the day of danger, if it shall come—and having done all to stand.

Pray you then for the Spirit of Faith to believe really in God, and for the spirit of ghostly strength to obey God honestly. No man ever asked honestly for that Spirit but what he gained it at last. And no man ever gained it but what he found the truth of St. Peter's own words—"Who will harm you, if you be followers of what is good?"

IX

THE STORY OF JOSEPH

"I fear God." Genesis xlii. 18.

Did it ever seem remarkable to you, as it has seemed to me, how many chapters of the Bible are taken up with the history of Joseph—a young man who, on the most memorable occasion in his life, said "I fear God," and had no other argument to use?

Thirteen chapters of the book of Genesis are mainly devoted to the tale of this one young man. Doubtless his father Jacob's going down into Egypt, was one of the most important events in the history of the Jews: we might expect, therefore, to hear much about it. But what need was there to spend four chapters at least in detailing Joseph's meeting with his brethren, even to minute accounts of the speeches on both sides?

Those who will may suppose that this is the effect of mere chance. Let us have no such fancy. If we believe that a Divine Providence watched over the composition of those old Scriptures; if we believe that they were meant to teach, not only the Jews but all mankind; if we believe that they reveal, not merely some special God in whom the Jews believed, but the true and only God, Maker of heaven and earth; if we believe, with St. Paul, that every book of the Old Testament is inspired by God, and profitable for doctrine, for reproof, for correction, for instruction in righteousness, that the man of God may be perfect, thoroughly furnished unto all good works—if we believe this, I say, it must be worth our while to look carefully and reverently at a story which takes up so large a part of the Bible, and expect to find in it something which may help to make us perfect, and thoroughly furnish us unto all good works.

Now, surely when we look at this history of Joseph, we ought to see at the first glance that it is not merely a story about a young man, but about the common human relations—the ties which bind any and every man to other human beings round him. For is it not a story about a brother and brothers? about a son and a father, about a master and a servant? about a husband and a wife? about a subject and a sovereign? and how they all behaved to each other—some well and some ill—in these relations?

Surely it is so, and surely this is why the story of Joseph has been always so popular among innocent children and plain honest folk of all kinds; because it is so simply human and humane; and therefore it taught them far more than they could learn from many a lofty, or seemingly lofty, book of devotion, when it spoke to them of the very duties they had to fulfil, and the very temptations they had to fight against, as members of a family or as members of society. "One touch of Nature (says the poet) makes the whole world kin;" and the touches of nature in this story of Joseph make us feel that he and his brethren, and all with whom he had to do, are indeed kin to us; that their duty is our duty too—their temptations ours—that where they fell, we may fall—where they conquered we may conquer.

For what is the story? A young lad is thrown into every temptation possible for him. Joseph is very handsome. The Bible says so expressly; so we may believe it. He has every gift of body and mind. He is, as his story proves plainly, a very clever person, with a strange power of making every one whom he deals with love him and obey him—a terrible temptation, as all God's gifts are, if abused by a man's vanity, or covetousness or ambition. He is an injured man too. He has been basely betrayed by his brothers; he is under a terrible temptation, to which ninety-nine men out of one hundred would have yielded—do yield, alas! to this day, to revenge himself if he ever has an opportunity. He is an injured man in Egypt, for he is a slave to a foreigner who has no legal or moral right over him. If ever there was a man who might be excused for cherishing a burning indignation against his oppressors, for brooding over his own wrongs, for despairing of God's providence, it is Joseph in Egypt. What could we do but pity him if he had said to himself, as thousands in his place have said since, "There is no God, or if there is, He does not care for me—He does not care what men do. He looks on unmoved at wrong and cruelty, and lets man do even as he will. Then why should not I do as I will? What are these laws of God of which men talk? What are these sacred bonds of family and society? Every one for himself is the rule of the world, and it shall be my rule. Every man's hand has been against me; why should not my hand be against every man? I have been betrayed; why should not I betray? I have been opprest; why should not I oppress? I have a lucky chance, too, of enjoying and revenging myself at the same time; why should I not take my good luck, and listen to the words of the tempter?"

My dear friends, this is the way in which thousands have talked, in which thousands talk to this day. This is the spirit which ends in breaking up society, as happened in France eighty years ago, in the inward corruption of a nation, and at last, in outward revolution and anarchy, from which may God in His mercy deliver us and our fellow-countrymen, and the generations yet to come. But any nation or any man, will only be delivered from it, as Joseph was delivered from it, by saying, "I fear God." No doubt it is most natural for a man who is injured and opprest to think in that way. Most natural—just as it is most natural for the trapped dog to struggle vainly, and, in his blind rage, bite at everything around him, even at his own master's hand when it offers to set him free. And if men are to be mere children of nature, like the animals, and not children of grace and sons of God, like Joseph, and like one greater than Joseph, then I suppose they must needs tear each other to pieces in envy and revenge, for there is nought better to be done. But if they wish to escape from the misery and ruin which envy and revenge bring with them, then they had better recollect that they are not children of nature, but children of God—they had best follow Joseph's example, and say, "I fear God."

For this poor, betrayed, enslaved lad had got into his heart something above Nature—something which Nature cannot give, but only the inspiration of the Spirit of God gives. He had got into his heart the belief that God's laws were sacred things and must not be broken, and that whatever befel him he must fear God. However unjust and lawless the world looked, God's laws were still in it, and over it, and would avenge themselves, and he must obey them at all risks. And what were God's laws in Joseph's opinion?

These—the common relations of humanity between master to servant, and servant to master; between parent to child, and child to parent; brother to brother and sister to sister, and between the man who is trusted and the man who trusts him. These laws were sacred; and if all the rest of the world broke them, he (Joseph) must not. He was bound to his master, not only by any law of man, but by the Law of God. His master trusted him, and left all that he had in his hand, and to Joseph the law of honour was the law of God. Then he must be justly faithful to his master. A sacred trust was laid on him, and to be true to it was to fear God.

After a while his master's wife tempts him. He refuses; not merely out of honour to his master, but from fear of God. "How can I do this great wickedness," says Joseph, "and sin against God?" His master and his mistress are heathen, but their marriage is of God nevertheless; the vow is sacred, and he must deny himself anything, endure anything, dare any danger of a dreadful death, and a prison almost as horrible probably as death itself, rather than break it.

So again, in the prison. If ever man had excuse for despairing of God's providence, for believing that right-doing did not pay, it was poor Joseph in that prison. But no. God is with him still. He believes still in the justice of God, the providence of God, and therefore he is cheerful, active—he can make the best even of a dungeon. He can find a duty to do even there; he can make himself useful, helpful, till the keeper of the prison too leaves everything in his hand.

What a gallant man! you say. Yes, my friends, but what makes him gallant? That which St. Paul says (in Hebrews xi.) made all the old Jewish heroes gallant—faith in God; real and living belief that God is—and that He is the rewarder of them that diligently seek Him.

At last Joseph's triumph comes. He has his reward. God helps him—because he will help himself. He is made a great officer of state, married to a woman of high rank, probably a princess, and he sees his brothers who betrayed him at his mercy. Their lives are in his hand at last. What will he do? Will he be a bad brother because they were bad? Or will he keep to his old watchword, "I fear God?" If he is tempted to revenge himself, he crushes the temptation down. He will bring his brothers to repentance. He will touch their inward witness, and make them feel that they have been wicked men. That is for their good. And strangely, but most naturally, their guilty consciences go back to the great sin of their lives—to Joseph's wrong, though they have no notion that Joseph is alive, much less near them. "Did I not tell you," says Reuben, "sin not against the lad, and ye would not hearken? Therefore is this distress come upon us."

Joseph punishes Simeon by imprisonment. It may be that he had reasons for it which we are not told. But when his brothers have endured the trial, and he finds that Benjamin is safe, he has nothing left but forgiveness. They are his brethren still—his own flesh and blood. And he "fears God." He dare not do anything but forgive them. He forgives them utterly, and welcomes them with an agony of happy tears. He will even put out of their minds the very memory of their baseness. "Now, therefore, be not grieved nor angry with yourselves that ye sold me hither, he says; for God sent me before you, to save your lives with a great deliverance."

Is not that Divine? Is not that the Spirit of God and of Christ? I say it is. For what is it but the likeness of Christ, who says for ever, out of heaven, to all mankind, "Be not grieved nor angry with yourselves that ye crucified me. For God, my Father, sent me to save your souls by a great salvation."

My friends, learn from this story of Joseph, and the prominent place in the Bible which it occupies—learn, I say, how hateful to God are family quarrels; how pleasant to God are family unity and peace, and mutual trust, and duty, and helpfulness. And if you think that I speak too strongly on this point, recollect that I do no more than St. Paul does, when he sums up the most lofty and mystical of all his Epistles, the Epistle to the Ephesians, by simple commands to husbands and wives, parents and children, masters and servants, as if he should say,—You wish to be holy? you wish to be spiritual? Then fulfil these plain family duties, for they, too, are sacred and divine, and he who despises them, despises the ordinances of God. And if you despise the laws of God, they will surely avenge themselves on you. If you are bad husbands or bad wives, bad parents or bad children, bad brothers or sisters, bad masters or servants, you will smart for it, according to the eternal laws of God, which are at work around you all day long, making the sinner punish himself whether he likes or not.

Examine yourselves—ask yourselves, each of you, Have I been a good brother? have I been a good son? have I been a good husband? have I been a good father? have I been a good servant? If not, all professions of religion will avail me nothing. If not, let me confess my sins to God, and repent and amend at once, whatever it may cost me. The fulfilling these plain duties is the true test of my faith, the true sign and test whether I really believe in God and in Jesus Christ our Lord. Do I believe that the world is Christ's making? and that Christ is governing it? Do I believe that these plain family relationships are Christ's sacred appointments? Do I believe that our Lord Jesus was made very man of the substance of His mother, to sanctify these family relationships, and claim them as the ordinances of God His Father?

In one word—copy Joseph; and when you are tempted say with Joseph, "Can I do this great wickedness, and sin—not against this man or this woman, but against—God."

Take home these plain, practical words. Take them home, and fear God at your own firesides. For at the last day, the Bible tells us, the Lord Jesus Christ will not reward you and me according to the opinions we held while in this mortal body, whether they were quite right or quite wrong, but according to the deeds which we did in the body, whether they were good or bad.

X

SLAVES OF FREE?

"Fear ye not, stand still, and see the salvation of the Lord, which he will show to you to-day: for the Egyptians whom ye have seen to day, ye shall see them again no more for ever. The Lord shall fight for you, and ye shall hold your peace."—Exodus xiv. 13, 14.

Why did God bring the Jews out of Egypt? God Himself told them why. To fulfil the promise which He made to Abraham, their forefather, that of his children He would make a great nation.

Now the Jews in Egypt were not a nation at all. A nation is free, governed by its own laws, one body of people, held together by one fellow feeling, one language, one blood, one religion; as we English are. We are a nation. The Jews were none in Egypt, no more than Negro slaves in America were a nation. They served a people of a different blood, as the Jews did in Egypt. They had no laws of their own; they had no fellow-feeling with each other, which enabled them to make common cause together, and help each other, and free each other.

Selfishness and cowardice make some men slaves. Above all, ungodliness makes men slaves. For when men do not fear and obey God, they are sure to obey their own lusts and passions, and become slaves to them. They become ready to sell themselves soul and body for money, or pleasure, or food. And their fleshly lusts, their animal appetites, keep them down, selfish, divided, greedy, and needy, at the mercy of those who are stronger and cunninger than themselves, just as the Jews were kept down by the strong and cunning Egyptians.

They had slavish hearts in them, and as long as they had, God could not make them into a nation. The Jews had slaves' hearts in them. They were glad enough to get free out of Egypt, to escape from their heavy labour in brick and mortar, from being oppressed, beaten, killed at the will and fancy of the Egyptians, from having their male children thrown into the river as soon as they were born, to keep them from becoming too numerous. They were glad enough, poor wretches, to escape from all their misery and oppression of which we read in the first three chapters of Exodus. But if they could do that, that was all they cared for. They did not want to be made wise, righteous, strong, free-hearted—they did not care about being made into a nation. We read that when by the Red Sea shore (Exodus xiv.), they saw themselves in great danger, the army of Pharaoh, King of Egypt, following close upon them to attack them, they lost heart at once, and were sore afraid, and cried unto Moses, "Is not this the word which we did tell thee in Egypt, saying, Let us alone that we may serve the Egyptians? For it had been better for us to serve the Egyptians than to die in the wilderness."

Cowards and slaves! The thing they feared above all, you see, was death. If they could but keep the miserable life in their miserable bodies, they cared for nothing beyond. They were willing to see their children taken from them and murdered, willing to be beaten, worked like dumb beasts for other men's profit, willing to be idolaters, heathens, worshipping the false gods of Egypt, dumb beasts and stocks and stones, willing to be despised, wretched, helpless slaves—if they could but keep the dear life in them. God knows there are plenty like them now-a-days—plenty who do not care how mean, helpless, wicked, contemptible they are, if they can but get their living by their meanness.

"But a man must live," says some one. How often one hears that made the excuse for all sorts of meanness, dishonesty, grasping tyranny. "A man must live!" Who told you that? It is better to die like a man than to live like a slave, and a wretch, and a sinner. Who told you that, I ask again? Not God's Bible, surely. Not the example of great and good men. If Moses had thought that, do you think he would have gone back from Midian, when he was in safety and comfort, with a wife and home, and children at his knee, and leave all he had on earth to face Pharaoh and the Egyptians, to face danger, perhaps a cruel death in shame and torture, and all to deliver his countrymen out of Egypt? Moses would sooner die like a man helping his countrymen, than live on the fat of the land while they were slaves. And forty years before he had shown the same spirit too, when though he was rich and prosperous, and high in the world, the adopted son of King Pharaoh's daughter (Exodus ii. 11), he disdained to be a slave and to see his countrymen slaves round him. We read how he killed an Egyptian, who was ill-treating one of his brothers, the Jews—and how he then fled out of Egypt into Midian, houseless and friendless, esteeming as St. Paul says, "the reproach of Christ"—that is the affliction and ill-will which came on him for doing right, "better than all the treasures of Egypt" (Heb xi. 24-27).

A man must live? The valiant Tyrolese of old did not say that (more than seventy years ago), when they fought to the last drop of their blood to defend their country against the French invaders. They were not afraid to die for liberty; and therefore they won honour from all honourable men, praise from all whose praise is worth having for ever.

A man must live? The old Greeks and Romans, heathens though they were, were above so mean a speech as that. They used to say, it was the noblest thing that can befall a man to die—not to live in clover, eating and drinking at his ease—to die among the foremost, fighting for wife and child and home.

A man must live? The martyrs of old did not say that, when they endured the prison and the scourge, the sword and the fire, and chose rather to die in torments unspeakable than deny the Lord Jesus who bought them with His blood, rather than do what they knew to be wrong. (Hebrews xi.) They were not afraid of torture and death; but of doing wrong they were unspeakably afraid. They were free, those holy men of old, truly free—free from their own love of ease and cowardice and selfishness, and all that drags a man down and makes a slave of him. They knew that "life is more than meat, and the body more than raiment." What matter if a man gain the whole world and lose his own soul? Their souls were free whatever happened to their bodies—the tormentor could not touch them, because they believed in God, because they did not fear those who could kill the body, and after that had no more that they could do.

And do you not see that a coward can never be free, never be godly, never be like Christ? For by a coward I mean not merely a man who is afraid of pain and trouble. Every one is that more or less. Jesus Himself was afraid when He cried in agony, "Father, if thou be willing, remove this cup from me: nevertheless not my will, but thine, be done." (Luke xxii. 42.) But a coward is a man who is so much afraid that to escape pain and danger, he will do what he ought not—do what he is ashamed of doing—do what lowers him; and therefore our Lord Jesus had perfect courage when He tasted death for all men, and endured the very agony from which He shrank, and while He said, "Father, if it be possible, let this cup pass," said also, "Nevertheless not my will, but Thine, be done."

The Jews were cowards when they cried, "Let us alone that we may serve the Egyptians." While a man is in that pitiful mood he cannot rise, he cannot serve God—for he must remain the slave of his own body, of which he is so mightily careful, the slave of his own fears, the slave of his own love of bodily comfort. Such a man does not dare serve God. He dare not obey God, when obeying God is dangerous and unpleasant. He dare not claim his heavenly birthright, his share in God's Spirit, his share in Christ's kingdom, because that would bring discomfort on him, because he will have to give up the sins he loves, because he will have to endure the insults and ill-will of wicked men. Thus cowards can never be free, for it is only where the Spirit of God is that there is liberty.

But the Jews were not yet fit to be made soldiers of. God would not teach them at once not to be afraid of men. He did not command them to turn again and fight these Egyptians, neither did He lead them into the land of Canaan the strait and short road, through the country of the Philistines, lest they should be discouraged when they saw war.

Now what was God's plan for raising the Jews out of this cowardly, slavish state? First, and above all, to make them trust in Him. While they were fearing the Egyptians, they could never fear Him. While they were fearing the Egyptians, they were ready to do every base thing, to keep their masters in good humour with them. God determined to teach them to fear Him more than they feared the Egyptians. God taught them that He was stronger than the Egyptians, for all their civilisation and learning and armies, chariots and horsemen, swords and spears. He would not let the Jews fight the Egyptians. He told them by the mouth of Moses, "Stand you still, and the Lord shall fight for you," and he commanded Moses to stretch out his rod over the sea. (Exodus xiv.) The Egyptians were stronger than the Jews—they would have cut them to pieces if they had come to a battle. For free civilised men like the Egyptians are always stronger than slaves, like the Jews; they respect themselves more, they hold together better, they have order and discipline, and obedience to their generals, which slaves have not. God intended to teach the Jews that also in His good time. But not yet. They were not fit yet to be made soldiers. They were not even men yet, but miserable slaves. A man is only a true man when he trusts in God, and none but God—when he fears God and nothing but God. And that was the lesson which God had to teach them. That was the lesson which He taught them by bringing them up out of Egypt by signs and wonders, that God was the Lord, God was their deliverer, God was their King—that let them be as weak as they might, He was strong—that if they could not fight the Egyptians God could overwhelm them—that if they could not cross the sea, God could open the sea to let them pass through. If they dreaded the waste howling wilderness of sand, with its pillars of cloud and fire, its stifling winds which burn the life out of man and beast, God could make the sand storms and the fire pillars and the deadly east wind of the desert work for their deliverance. And so He taught them to fear Himself, to trust in Him, to look up to Him as their deliverer whose strength was shown most gloriously when they were weakest and most despairing.

This was the great lesson which God meant to teach the children of Israel, that the root and ground of all other lessons, is that this earth belongs to the Lord alone. That had been what God had been teaching them already, by the plagues of Egypt. The Egyptians worshipped their great river Nile, and thought it was a god, and the Lord turned the Nile water into blood, and showed that He could do what He liked with it. The Egyptians worshipped dumb beasts and insects, and fancied in their folly that they were gods. The Lord sent plagues of frogs and flies and locusts, and took them away again when He liked, to show them that the beasts and creeping things were His also.

The Egyptians worshipped false gods who as they fancied managed the seasons and the weather. God sent them thunder and hail when it pleased Him, and showed the Jews that He, not these false gods of Egypt, ruled the heavens. The Egyptians and many other heathen nations of the earth used to offer their children to false gods. I do not mean by killing them in sacrifice, but by naming them after some idol, and then expecting that the idol would ever afterwards prosper and strengthen them. Thus the kings were called after the sun. Pharaoh means the Sun-king; for they fancied that the sun was a god, and protected their kings one after the other. And God slew all the first-born of Egypt, even the first-born of King Pharaoh on his throne. The Sun-god could not help him. The idols of Egypt could not take care of their worshippers—only the children of the Jews escaped. (Exodus xii.) What a lesson for the Jews! And they needed it; for during the four hundred years that they had been in Egypt they had almost forgotten the one true God, the God of their forefathers, Abraham, Isaac and Jacob; at least they thought Him no better than the false gods of Egypt. After all these wondrous proofs of God's almighty power, and His jealousy for His own name, they fell away to idols again and again. They worshipped a golden calf in Horeb (Exodus xxxii.); they turned aside to worship the idols of the nations whom they passed through on their way to Canaan. Idolatry had been rooted in their hearts, and it took many years of severe training and teaching on God's part to drive it out of them—to make them feel that the one God, who made heaven and earth, had delivered them—that they belonged to Him, that they had a share in Him—to make them join with one heart and voice in the glorious song of Moses:

"I will sing unto the Lord, for he hath triumphed gloriously: the horse and his rider hath he thrown into the sea. The Lord is my strength and song and he is become my salvation: he is my God and I will prepare him an habitation; my father's God, and I will exalt him. The Lord is a man of war: the Lord is his name. Pharaoh's chariots and his host hath he cast into the sea: his chosen captains also are drowned in the Red Sea. The depths have covered them: they sank into the bottom as a stone. Thy right hand, O Lord, is become glorious in power: thy right hand, O Lord, hath dashed in pieces the enemy. And in the greatness of thine excellency thou hast overthrown them that rose up against thee: thou sentest forth thy wrath, which consumed them as stubble. And with the blast of thy nostrils the waters were gathered together, the floods stood upright as an heap, and the depths were congealed in the heart of the sea. The enemy said, I will pursue, I will overtake, I will divide the spoil; my lust shall be satisfied upon them; I will draw my sword, my hand shall deliver them. Thou didst blow with thy wind, the sea covered them: they sank as lead in the mighty waters. Who is like unto thee, O Lord, among the gods? who is like thee, glorious in holiness, fearful in praises, doing wonders? Thou stretchedst out thy right hand, the earth swallowed them. Thou in thy mercy hast led forth the people which thou hast redeemed: thou hast guided them in thy strength unto thy holy habitation. The people shall hear, and be afraid: sorrow shall take hold on the inhabitants of Palestina. Then the dukes of Edom shall be amazed; the mighty men of Moab, trembling shall take hold upon them; all the inhabitants of Canaan shall melt away. Fear and dread shall fall upon them; by the greatness of thine arm they shall be as still as a stone; till thy people pass over, O Lord, till the people pass over, which thou hast purchased. Thou shalt bring them in and plant them in the mountain of thine inheritance, in the place, O Lord, which thou hast made for thee to dwell in, in the Sanctuary, O Lord, which thy hands have established. The Lord shall reign for ever and ever. For the horse of Pharaoh went in with his chariots and with his horsemen into the sea, and the Lord brought again the waters of the sea upon them; but the children of Israel went on dry land in the midst of the sea." (Exodus xv. 1-19.)

This was God's first lesson to the Jews; the first step towards making them a free nation. For believe me, my friends, the only thought which can make men feel free and strong, the only thought which can keep them from being afraid of each other, afraid of the seasons, and the elements, and the chances and changes of this mortal life, the only thought which can teach them that they are brothers, bound together to help and love each other, in short the only thought which can make men citizens—is the thought that the one God is their Father, and that they are all His children—that they have one God, one religion, one baptism, one Lord and Saviour, who has delivered them, and will deliver them again and again from all their sins and miseries; one God and Father of all, who is in all, and for all, and over all, to whom they all owe equal duty, in whom they all have an equal share.

That lesson God began to teach the Jews by the Red Sea. That lesson God has taught our English forefathers again and again; and that lesson He will teach us, their children, as often as we forget it, by signs and wonders, by chastisements and by mercies, till we all learn to trust in Him and Him only, and know that there is none other name under heaven by which we can be saved from evil in this life or in the life to come, but the name of Jesus Christ, the Son of God, the Angel of the Covenant, who led the Jews up out of the land of Egypt.

XI

DANGERS—AND THE LITANY

"Then they cried unto the Lord in their trouble, and he delivered them out of their distresses. And he led them forth by the right way, that they might go to a city of habitation. Oh that men would praise the Lord for his goodness, and for his wonderful works to the children of men."—Psalm cvii. 6-8.

This 107th Psalm is a noble psalm—a psalm which has given comfort to thousands in suffering and in danger, even in the sorrows which they have brought on themselves by their own folly. For it tells them of a Lord who hears them when they cry to Him in their trouble, and who delivers them from their distress.

It was written on a special occasion, as all the most important words of the Bible are written—written seemingly, after some band of Jews struggling across the desert, on their return from the captivity in Babylon, had been in great danger of death. They went astray in the wilderness out of their way, and found no city to rest in; hungry and thirsty their soul fainted in them, so they cried unto the Lord in their trouble, and He delivered them from their distress. He led them forth by the right way, that they might go to the city where they dwelt. That was the plain fact, on which the psalmist built up this noble psalm.

In the blazing sandy desert, without water, food, or shade, they had lost their path, and were at their wit's end. And they cried unto the Lord their God for guidance, for they could not guide themselves. And the Lord answered their prayer and guided them. We do not read that God worked a miracle for them, or sent an angel to lead them. Simply, somehow or other, they found their way after all, and got safe out of the desert; and they believed that it was God who enabled them to find their way, and praised the Lord for His goodness; and for His goodness not only to them, but to the children of men—to all men who had the sense to call on Him in trouble, and to put themselves in their right place as men—God's children, calling for help to their Father in heaven.

Therefore the psalmist goes on to speak of the cases of God's goodness, which he seems to have seen, or at least heard of. Of wretched prisoners, bound fast in misery and iron, and that through their own fault and folly, who had cried unto the Lord in their trouble, and been delivered by Him from the darkness of the dungeon. Of foolish men who had ruined their health, or at least their prospects in life, by their own sin and folly, till their soul abhorred all manner of meat, and they were hard at death's door. But of them, too, he says, when they cried unto the Lord in their trouble, He delivered them from their distress. He sent His word—what we now foolishly call the laws of Nature, but which the Psalmist knew to be the ever-working power and providence of God—and healed them, and they were saved from their destruction.

Then he goes on to speak of the dangers of the sea which were especially strange and terrible to him—a Jew. For the Jews were no sailors; and if they went to sea, would go as merchants, or supercargoes in ships manned by heathens; and the danger was really great. The ships were clumsy; navigation was ill-understood; the storms of the Mediterranean sea were then as now, sudden and furious; and when one came on, the heathen sailors would, I doubt not, be at their wit's end, their courage melting away because of the trouble, and call on all their gods and idols to help them; but the men of whom the Psalmist speaks, though they were no seamen, knew on whom to call. It was by the word of the Lord that the stormy wind arose which lifted up the billows. He could quell the storm if He would, and when He would; and to Him they cried and not in vain. "And He made the storm to cease so that the waves thereof were still. Then were they glad, because they were at rest, and so He brought them to the haven where they would be."

My friends, this was the simple faith of the old Jews. And this was the simple faith of our forefathers by land and sea. And this faith, as I believe, made England great. The faith that there was a living God, a living Lord, who would hear the cry of poor creatures in their trouble, even when they had brought their trouble on themselves. Our forefathers were not mere landsmen like the Jews, but the finest seamen the world has ever seen. And yet they were not ashamed in storm and danger to cry like the Jews unto the Lord, that He might make the storm to cease, and bring them to the haven where they would be. Yes! faith in God did not make them the less brave, skilful, cautious, scientific; and it need not make us so. Skill and science need not take away our faith in God. I trust it will not take it away, and I believe it will not take it away, as long as we can hear what I once heard, on board of one of the finest men of war[1] in

[1] H.M.S. the Duke of Wellington.

the British Navy—the ship in which and from which, all British sailors may learn their duty—when I saw some six or eight hundred men mustered on the deck for daily morning prayer, and heard the noble old prayer, which our forefathers have handed down to us, to be said every day in Her Majesty's navy:[2]

"O eternal God who alone spreadest out the heavens, and rulest the raging of the sea; who hast compassed the waters with bounds, until day and night come to an end; be pleased to receive into Thy Almighty and most gracious protection, the persons of us Thy servants, and the fleet in which we serve. Preserve us from the dangers of the sea, and from the violence of the enemy, that we may be a safeguard unto our most gracious Sovereign Lady Queen Victoria and her dominions, and a security for such as pass on the seas upon their lawful occasions; that the inhabitants of our island may in peace and quietness serve Thee our God, and that we may return in safety to enjoy the blessings of the land, with the fruits of our labours, and with a thankful remembrance of Thy mercies, to praise and glorify Thy holy name; through Jesus Christ our Lord. Amen."

Then, as I stood upon that deck, and heard that solemn appeal to God, before each man went about his appointed duty for the day, said I to myself, "The ancient spirit is not dead. It may be that it is sleeping in these prosperous times. But it is not dead, as long as this nation by those prayers confesses that we ought at least to believe in a God who hears our prayers, by land and sea. Those grand words were perhaps nothing but a form to most of the men who heard them. But they were a form which bore witness to a truth which was true, even if they forgot it—a truth which they might need some day, and feel the need of, and cling to, as the sailors of old time clung to it. Those words would surely sink into the men's ears, and some day, it might be, bear fruit in their hearts. In storm, in wreck, in battle, and in the hour of death, and in the day of judgment, these words would surely rise in many a brave fellow's memory, and help him to do his duty like a man, because there was a living Lord and God above him who knew his weakness and would hear his prayers."

And we, my friends, here safe on land, we have a national prayer, or rather a series of prayers, to Christ as God, which ought to remind us of that noble truth which the 107th Psalm is meant to teach. You hear it all of you every Sunday morning. I mean the Litany. That noble composition, which seems to me more wise as a work of theology, more beautiful as a work of art, the oftener I use

[2] Form of prayer to be used at sea.

it—That Litany, I say, is modelled on the 107th Psalm; and it expresses the very heart and spirit of our forefathers three hundred years ago. It bids us pray to be delivered from every conceivable harm, to Father, Son, and Holy Spirit. And then it prays for every conceivable blessing, not only for each of us separately, but for this whole nation of England, Great Britain, and Ireland, and for all the nations on earth, and for the heathen and the savage.

Of course, just because it is a National prayer, and meant for all Englishmen alike, all of it does not suit each and every one of us at the same time. Each heart knows its own bitterness. Each soul has its own special mercy to ask. But there is a word in the Litany here, and another there, which will fit each of us in turn, if we will but follow it. One may have to pray to be delivered from pride, vain-glory, and hypocrisy—another to be delivered from foul living and deadly sin—another to be delivered, or to have those whom he loves delivered, from battle, murder, and sudden death. Another to be delivered from the dangers of affliction and tribulation; another from the far worse danger of wrath; but all have to pray to be delivered from something. And all have to pray to the same deliverer—Christ, who was born a Man, died a man, and rose again a man, that He might know what was in man, and be able to succour those who are tempted, seeing that He was tempted in all things like as we are, yet without sin.

But there is a part—the latter part—of that Litany which, I think, many do not understand or feel. Perhaps they have reason to thank God that they do not understand or feel it; yet, the day may come—a day of sadness, fear, perplexity, sorrow, when they will understand it, and thank God that their forefathers placed it in the prayer-book, for them to fall back upon, as comfort and hope in the day of trouble; putting words into their mouths and thoughts into their hearts, which they, perhaps, never would have found out for themselves.

I mean that latter part of the Litany which talks of the evils which the craft and subtilty of the devil or men work against us, that they may be brought to nought, and by the providence of God's goodness be dispersed, that we may be hurt by no persecutions—which calls on Christ to arise and deliver us, for His name's sake and His honour, which pleads before God the noble works which He did in the days of our forefathers; and which continues with short prayers, almost cries, which have something in them of terror, almost of agony. What have such words to do with us? Why are they put into the mouths of us English, safe, comfortable, prosperous, above almost all the nations upon earth?

Ah! my friends, those prayers, when they were first put into our prayer-book, were spoken for the hearts of Englishmen. They were not prayers for one afflicted person here, and another there,—they, too, were National prayers. They were the cries of the English nation in agony—in the time when, three hundred years ago, the mightiest nations and powers of Europe, temporal and spiritual, were set against this little isle of England, and we expected not merely to be invaded and conquered, but destroyed utterly and horribly with sword and fire, by the fleets and armies of the King of Spain. In that great danger and war our forefathers cried to God; and they cried all the more earnestly, because they felt that their hands were not clean; that they had plenty and too many sins to be "mercifully forgiven," and that at best they could but ask God "mercifully to look upon their infirmities," and, "for the glory of His name, turn from them those evils which they most righteously had deserved." But nevertheless they cried unto God in their great agony, because they had the spirit of the old Psalmist, who said, "They cried unto the Lord in their trouble, and He delivered them out of their distress."

And what answer God made to their prayers all the world knows, or should know. For if He had not answered their prayer, we should not be here this day, a great, and strong, and prosperous nation, with a pure Church and a free Gospel, and the Holy Bible if he wills, in the hands of the poorest child. Unless prayer be a dream, and there be no God in heaven worth calling a God—then did God answer the prayers of our forefathers three hundred years ago, when they cried unto Him as one nation in their utter need.

But some will say—this may be all very true and very fine, but we are in no such utter need now. Why should we use those prayers?

My dear friends, let me say, if you are not now in utter need, in terror, anxiety, danger, if you have no need to cry to Christ, "Graciously look upon our afflictions; pitifully behold the sorrows of our hearts," how do you know that there is not some one in any and every congregation who is? And you and I, if we have said the Litany in spirit and in truth, have been praying for them. The Litany bids us speak as members of a Church, as citizens of a nation, bound together by the ties of blood and of laws, as well as self-interest. The Litany bids us say, not selfishly and apart, Graciously look on my afflictions, but on our afflictions—the afflictions of every English man, and woman, and child, who is in trouble, or ever will be in trouble hereafter. Oh, remember this last word. Generations long since dead and buried have prayed for you, and God has heard their prayers; and now you have been praying for your children, and your children's children, and generations yet unborn, that, if ever a dark day should come over England, a time of want and danger and perplexity and misery, God would deliver them in their turn out of their distress. And more; you have been teaching your children, that they may teach their children in turn, and pray and cry to God in their trouble; and thus this grand old Litany is to us, and to those we shall leave behind us a precious National heir-loom, teaching us and them the lesson of the 107th Psalm—that there is a Lord in heaven who hears the prayers of men, the sinful as well as the sorrowful, that when they cry unto the Lord in their trouble, He delivers them out of their distress, and that men should therefore praise the Lord for His goodness, and declare the wonders which He doeth for the children of men.

XII

WILD TIMES

OR

DAVID'S FAITH IN A LIVING GOD

"David therefore departed thence, and escaped to the cave Adullam: and when his brethren and all his father's house heard it, they went down thither to him. And every one that was in distress, and every one that was in debt, and every one that was discontented, gathered themselves unto him; and he became a captain over them: and there were with him about four hundred men."—
1 Sam. xxii. 1, 2.

In every country, at some time or other, there have been evil days—days of violence, tyranny, misrule, war, invasion, when men are too apt, for want of settled law, to take the law into their own hands; and the land is full of robbers, outlaws, bands of partizans and irregular soldiers—wild times, in which wild things are done.

Of such times we here in England have had no experience, and we forget how common they are; we forget that many great nations have been in this state again and again. We forget that almost all Europe was in that wild and lawless state in our fathers' times, and therefore we forget that the Bible, which tells man his whole duty, must needs tell men about such times as those, and how a man may do his duty, and save his soul therein. For the Bible is every man's book, and has its lesson for every man. It is meant not merely for comfortable English folk, who sit at home at ease, under just laws and a good government. It is meant just as much for the opprest, for the persecuted, for the man who is fighting for his country, for the man who has been found fighting in vain, and is simply waiting for God's help, and crying, "Lord, how long? how long ere Thou avenge the blood that is shed?" It is meant as much for such as for you and me; that every man, in whatever fearful times he may live, and whatever fearful trials he may go through, and whatever fearful things he may be tempted to do, and, indeed, may have to do, in self-defence, may still be able to go to the Bible, there to find light for his feet, and a lantern for his path, and so that he may steer through the worst of times by Faith in the Living God.

Again, such lawless times are certain to raise up bold and adventurous men, more or less like David. Men of blood—who are yet not altogether bad men—who are forced to take the law into their own hands, to try and keep their countrymen together, to put down tyrants and robbers, and to drive out invaders. And men, too, suffering from deep and cruel wrongs, who are forced for their lives' sake, and their honour's sake, to escape—to flee to the mountains and the forests, and to foreign lands, and there live as they can till times shall be better. There have been such men in all wild times—outlaws, chiefs of armed bands, like our Robin Hood, whose name was honoured in England for hundreds of years as the protector of the poor and the opprest, and the punisher of the Norman tyrants: a man made up of much good and much evil, whom we must not judge, but when we think of him, only thank God that we do not live in such times now, when no man's life or property, or the honour of his family was safe.

Such men, too, in our fathers' days, were the Tyrolese heroes, Hofer and the Good Monk who left, the one his farm and the other his cloister, to lead their countrymen against the invading French; men of blood, who were none the less men of God. And such is, in our own days, that famous Garibaldi, whose portrait hangs in many an English cottage, for a proof that though we, thank God, do not need such men in peaceful England, our hearts bid us to love and honour them wherever they be. There have been such men in all bad times, and there will be till the world's end, and they will do great deeds, and their names will be famous, and often honoured and adored by men.

Now, what does the Bible say of such men? Does it give any rule by which we may judge them? any rule which they ought to obey? Can God's blessing be on them? Can they obey God in that wild and dark and dangerous station to which He seems to have called them—to which God certainly called Hofer and the Good Monk?

I think if the Bible did not answer that question it would not be a complete book—if it spoke only of peaceful folk, and peaceful times; when, alas! from the beginning of the world, the earth has been but too full of violence and misrule, war and desolation. But the Bible does answer that question. A large portion of one whole book is actually taken up with the history of a young outlaw—of David, the shepherd boy, who rises through strange temptations and dangers to be a great king, the first man who, since Moses, formed the Jews into one strong united nation. It does not hide his faults, even his fearful sins, but it shows us that he had a right road to follow, though he often turned aside from it. It shows us that he could be a good man if he chose, though he was an outlaw at the head of a band of ruffians; and it shows us the secret of his power and of his success—Faith in the Living God.

Therefore it is that after the Bible has shown us (in the Book of Ruth) worthy Boaz standing among his reapers in the barley field, it goes on to show us Boaz's great-grandson, David, a worthy man likewise, but of a very different life, marked out by God from his youth for strange and desperate deeds; killing, as a mere boy, a lion and a bear, overthrowing the Philistine giant with a sling and a stone, captain of a band of outlaws in the wilderness, fighting battles upon battles; and at last a king, storming the mountain fortress of Jerusalem, and setting up upon Mount Zion, which shall never be removed, the Throne of David. A strange man, and born into a strange time. You all know the first part of David's history—how Samuel secretly anoints David king over Israel, and how the Spirit of the Lord comes from that day forward upon the young lad (1 Samuel xvi. 12). How king Saul meanwhile fell into dark and bad humours. How the Spirit of the Lord—of goodness and peace of mind—goes from him, and an evil spirit from the Lord troubles him. Then how young David is sent for to play to him on his harp (1 Samuel xvi.), and soothe his distempered mind. Already we hear of David as a remarkable person; we hear of his extraordinary beauty, his skill in music; we hear, too, how he is already a man of war, and a mighty valiant man, and prudent in matters, and the Lord is with him.

Then follows the famous story of his killing Goliath the Philistine (1 Samuel xvii.). Poor, distempered Saul, it seems, had forgotten him, though David had cured his melancholy with his harp-playing, and had actually been for a while his armour-bearer, for when he comes back with the giant's head, Saul has to ask Abner who he is; but after that he will let him go no more home to his father.

Then follows the beautiful story of Jonathan, Saul's gallant son (1 Samuel xviii.), and his love for David. Then of Saul's envy of David, and how, in a sudden fit of hatred, he casts his javelin at him. Then how he grows afraid of him, and makes him captain of a thousand men, and gives him his daughter, on condition of David's killing him two hundred Philistines. And how he goes on, capriciously, honouring David one day and trying to kill him the next. While David rises always, and all Israel and Judah love him, and he behaves himself more wisely than all the servants of Saul. At last comes the open rupture. Saul, after trying to murder David, sends assassins to his house, and David flees for his life once and for all. He has served his master Saul loyally and faithfully. There is no word of his having opposed Saul, set himself up against him, boasted of himself, or in any way brought his anger down upon him. Saul is his king, and David has been loyal and true to him. But Saul's envy has grown to hatred, and that to murder. He murders the priests, with all their wives and children, for having given bread and shelter to David. And now David must flee into the wilderness and set up for himself, and he flees to the cave of Adullam (1 Samuel xxii.); and there you see the Bible does not try to hide what David's position was, and what sort of men he had about him—his brethren and his father's house, who were afraid that Saul would kill them instead of him, after the barbarous Eastern fashion, and among them the three sons of Zeruiah, his sister; and everyone who was discontented, and everyone who was in debt, all the most desperate and needy—one can conceive what sort of men they must have been. The Bible tells us afterwards of the wicked men and men of Belial who were among them—wild men, with weapons in their hands, and nothing to prevent their becoming a band of brutal robbers, if they had not had over them a man in whom, in spite of all his faults, was the Spirit of God.

We must remember, meanwhile, that David had his temptations. He had been grievously wronged. Saul had returned him evil for good. All David's services and loyalty to Saul had been repaid with ingratitude and accusations of conspiracy against him. What terrible struggles of rage and indignation must have passed through David's heart! What a longing to revenge himself! He knew, too, for Samuel the prophet had told him, that he should be king one day. What a temptation, then, to make himself king at once! It was no secret either. The people knew of it. Jonathan, Saul's son, knew of it, and, in his noble, self-sacrificing way, makes no secret of it (1 Samuel xx.). What a temptation to follow the fashion which is too common in the East to this day, and strike down his tyrant at one blow, as many a man has done since, and to proclaim himself king of the Jews. Yes, David had heavy temptations—temptations which he could only conquer by faith in the Living God. And, because he masters himself, and remains patient and loyal to his king under every insult and wrong, he is able to master that wild and desperate band of men, and set them an example of patience and chivalry, loyalty and justice; to train them to be, not a terror and a scourge to the yeomen and peasants round, but a protection and a guard against the Philistines and Amalekites, and, in due time, his trusty bodyguard of warriors—men who have grown grey beside him through a hundred battles, who are to be the foundation of his national army, and help him to make the Jews one strong and united prosperous kingdom.

All this the shepherd lad has to do, and he does it, by faith in the Living God, and so makes himself for all ages to come the pattern of perfect loyalty. And now, let us take home this one lesson—That the secret of David's success is not his beauty, his courage, his eloquence, his genius; other men have had gifts from God as great as David's, and have misused them to their own ruin, and to the misery of their fellow-men. No; the secret of David's success is his faith in the Living God; and that will be the secret of our success. Without faith in God, the most splendid talents may lead a man to be a curse to himself and to his neighbours. With faith in God, a very common-place person, without any special cleverness, may do great things, and make himself useful and honoured in his generation.

XIII

DAVID AND NABAL

OR

SELF-CONTROL

"And David said to Abigail, Blessed be the Lord God of Israel, which sent thee this day to meet me: And blessed be thy advice, and blessed be thou, which hast kept me this day from coming to shed blood, and from avenging myself with mine own hand."—1 Samuel xxv. 32, 33.

The story of David and Nabal needs no explanation. It tells us of part of David's education—of a great lesson which he learnt—of a great lesson which we may learn. It is told with a dignity and a simplicity, with a grace and liveliness which makes itself understood at once, and carries its own lesson to any one who has a human heart in him.

"And there was a man in Maon, whose possessions were in Carmel"—the park grass upland with timber trees—not the northern Carmel where Elijah slew the prophets of Baal, but the southern one on the edge of the desert. "And the man was very great, and he had three thousand sheep, and a thousand goats: and he was shearing his sheep in Carmel. Now the name of the man was Nabal; and the name of his wife Abigail: and she was a woman of good understanding, and of a beautiful countenance: but the man was churlish and evil in his doings; and he was of the house of Caleb." Caleb was Joshua's friend, who had conquered all that land in Joshua's time. Nabal, therefore, had all the pride of a man of most ancient and noble family—and no shame to him if he had had a noble, courteous, and generous heart therewith, instead of being, as he was, a stupid and brutal person.

"And David heard in the wilderness that Nabal did shear his sheep. And David sent out ten young men, and David said unto the young men, Get you up to Carmel, and go to Nabal, and greet him in my name: And thus shall ye say unto him that liveth in prosperity, Peace be to thee, and peace be to thine house, and peace be to all that thou hast. And now I have heard that thou hast shearers: now thy shepherds which were with us, we hurt them not, neither was there ought missing unto them, all the while they were in Carmel. Ask the young men, and they will show thee. Wherefore let the young men find favour in thine eyes: for we come in a good day: give, I pray thee, whatsoever cometh to thine hand unto thy servants, and unto thy son David. And when David's young men came, they spake to Nabal, according to all thee words of David, and ceased."

Nabal refuses; and in a way that shows, as his wife says of him, how well his name fits him—a fool is his name, and folly is with him. Insolently and brutally he refuses, as fools are wont to do. "And Nabal answered David's servants, and said, Who is David? and who is the son of Jesse? there be many servants now-a-days that break away every man from his master. Shall I then take my bread, and my water, and my flesh that I have killed for my shearers, and give it unto men whom I know not whence they be?"

"As slaves break away from their master." This was an intolerable insult. To taunt a free-born man, as David was, with having been a slave and a runaway. It is hard to conceive how Nabal dared to say such a thing of a fierce chieftain like David, with six hundred armed men at his back; but there is no saying what a fool will not do when the spirit of the Lord is gone from him, and his own fancy and passions lead him captive.

So David's young men came and told David. "And David said to his men, Gird every man on his sword. And they girded on every man his sword; and David also girded on his sword: and there went up after David about four hundred men; and two hundred abode by the stuff."

That is a grand passage—grand, because it is true to human nature, true to the determined, prompt, kingly character of David. He does not complain, bluster, curse over the insult as a weak man might have done. He has been deeply hurt, and he is too high-minded to talk about it. He will do, and not talk. A dark purpose settles itself instantly in his mind. Perhaps he is ashamed of it, and dare not speak of it, even to himself. But what it was he confessed afterwards to Abigail, that he purposed utterly to kill Nabal and all his people. David was wrong of course. But the Bible makes no secret of the wrong-doings of its heroes. It does not tell us that they were infallible and perfect. It tells us that they were men of like passions with ourselves, in order that by seeing how they conquered their passions we may conquer ours.

Meanwhile, Nabal's young men, his servants and slaves, see the danger, and go to Abigail. "One of the young men told Abigail, saying, Behold, David sent messengers out of the wilderness to salute our master; and he railed on them. But the men were very good unto us, and we were not hurt, neither missed we any thing, as long as we were conversant with them, when we were in the fields: They were a wall unto us both by night and day, all the while we were with them keeping the sheep. Now therefore know and consider what thou wilt do; for evil is determined against our master, and against all his household: for he is such a son of Belial, that a man cannot speak to him. Then Abigail made haste, and took two hundred loaves, and two bottles of wine, and five sheep ready dressed, and five measures of parched corn, and an hundred clusters of raisins, and two hundred cakes of figs, and laid them on asses. And she said unto her servants, Go on before me; behold, I come after you. But she told not her husband Nabal."

And then follows the beautiful scene which has been the subject of many a noble picture. The fair lady kneeling before the terrible outlaw in the mountain woods, as she came down by the covert of the hill, and softening his fierce heart with her beauty and her eloquence and her prayers, and bringing him back to his true self—to forgiveness, generosity, and righteousness.

"And when Abigail saw David, she hasted, and lighted off the ass, and fell before David on her face, and bowed herself to the ground, and fell at his feet, and said, Upon me, my lord, let this iniquity be: and let thine handmaid, I pray thee, speak in thine audience, and hear the words of thine handmaid. Let not my lord, I pray thee, regard this man of Belial, even Nabal: for as his name is, so is he; Nabal is his name, and folly is with him; but I, thine handmaid, saw not the young men of my lord, whom thou didst send. Now therefore, my lord, as the Lord liveth, and as thy soul liveth, seeing the Lord hath withholden thee from coming to shed blood, and from avenging thyself with thine own hand, now let thine enemies, and they that seek evil to my lord, be as Nabal.... I pray thee forgive the trespass of thine handmaid: for the Lord will certainly make my lord a sure house; because my lord fighteth the battles of the Lord, and evil hath not been found in thee all thy days."

And she conquers. The dark shadow passes off David's soul, and he is again the true, chivalrous, God-fearing David, who has never drawn sword yet in his own private quarrel, but has committed his cause to God who judgeth righteously, and will, if a man abide patiently in Him, make his righteousness as clear as the light, and his just-dealing as the noonday. Frankly he confesses his fault. "Blessed be thy advice, and blessed be thou which has kept me this day from coming to shed blood, and from avenging myself with mine own hand. For in very deed, as the Lord God of Israel liveth, which has kept me back from hurting thee, except thou hadst hasted and come to meet me, surely there had not a man been left unto Nabal by the morning light." Then follows the end. Abigail goes back to Nabal. Then the bully shows himself a coward. The very thought of the danger which he has escaped is too much for him. His heart died within him. "And Abigail came to Nabal; and behold, he held a feast in his house like the feast of a king; and Nabal's heart was merry within him, for he was very drunken: wherefore she told him nothing less or more until the morning light. But it came to pass in the morning, when the wine was gone out of Nabal, and his wife had told him these things, that his heart died within him, and he became as a stone. And it came to pass, about ten days after, that the Lord smote Nabal, that he died." One can imagine the picture for oneself. The rich churl sitting there in the midst of all his slaves and his wealth as one thunderstruck, helpless and speechless, till one of those mysterious attacks, which we still rightly call a stroke, and a visitation of God, ends him miserably. And when he is dead, Abigail becomes the wife of David, and shares his fortunes and his dangers in the wilderness.

Now, what may we learn from this story? Surely what David learnt—the unlawfulness of revenge. David was to be trained to be a perfect king by learning self-control, and therefore he has to learn that he must not punish in his own quarrel. If he must not lift up his hand against Saul, on the ground of loyalty, neither must he lift up his hand against Nabal, on the deeper ground of justice and humanity.

But from whom did David learn this? From himself. From his own heart and conscience, enlightened by the Spirit of God. Abigail gave him no commandment from God, in the common sense of the word. She only put David in mind of what he knew already. She appeals to his known nobleness of mind, and takes for granted that he will hear reason—takes for granted that he will do right—and so brought him to himself again. The Lord was withholding him, she says, from coming to shed blood, and avenging himself with his own hand. But that would have been of no avail had there not been something in David's own heart which answered to her words. For the Spirit of God had not left David; and it was the Spirit of God which gave him nobleness of heart—the Spirit of God which made him answer, "Blessed be the Lord God of Israel who sent thee this day to meet me; and blessed be thy advice, and blessed be thou which hast kept me this day from shedding of blood."

Though Abigail did not pretend to bring a message from God, David felt that she had brought one. And she was in his eyes not merely a suppliant pleading for mercy, but a prophetess declaring to him a divine law which he dare not resist. "It has been said by them of old time," our blessed Lord tells us, "an eye for an eye, and a tooth for a tooth; thou shalt love thy neighbour and hate thine enemy." This is the first natural law which a savage lays down for himself. There is a rude sense of justice in it, mixed up with the same brute instinct of revenge which makes the wild beast turn in rage upon the hunter who wounds him. But our Lord Jesus Christ brings in a higher and more spiritual law. Punishment is to be left to the magistrate, who punishes in God's name. And where the law cannot touch the wrongdoer, God, who is the author of law, can and will punish. "Vengeance is mine, I will repay, saith the Lord." Yes! if punishment must be, then let God punish. Let man forgive. I say unto you, said our Lord, "Love your enemies. Do good to them that hate you—bless them that curse you—pray for them that despitefully use you and persecute you, that you may be the children of your Father which is in heaven, for He maketh His sun to shine upon the evil and the good, and sendeth rain on the just and the unjust."

It is a hard lesson. But we must learn it. And we shall learn it, just as far as we are guided by the Spirit of God, who forms in us the likeness of Christ. And men are learning it more and more in Christian lands. Wherever Christ's gospel is truly and faithfully preached, the fashion, of revenge is dying out. There are countries still in Christendom in which men think nothing every day of stabbing and shooting the man who has injured them; and far, very far, from Christ and His Spirit must they be still. But we may have hope for them; for if we look at home, it was not so very many years ago that any Englishman, who considered himself a gentleman, was bound by public opinion to fight a duel for any slight insult. It was not so many years ago that among labouring men brutal quarrels and open fights were common, and almost daily occurrences. But now men are learning more and more to control their tempers and their tongues, and find it more and more easy, and more pleasant and more profitable, as our Lord forewarned them when He said, "Take my yoke upon you and learn of me, for I am meek and lowly in heart, and ye shall find rest unto your souls, for my yoke is easy, and my burden is light." And Christ's easy yoke is the yoke of self-control, by which we bridle the passions which torment us. Christ's light burden is the burden and obligation laid on every one of us, to forgive others, even as God for Christ's sake has forgiven us. And the rest which shall come to our souls is the rest which David found, when he listened to the voice of God speaking by the lips of Abigail; the true and divine rest of heart and peace of mind—rest and peace from the inward storm of fretfulness, suspicion, jealousy, pride, wrath, revenge, which blackens the light of heaven to a man, and turns to gall and wormwood every blessing which God sends.

Ah! my friends, if ever that angry storm rises in our hearts, if ever we be tempted to avenge ourselves, and cast off the likeness of God for that of the savage, and return evil for evil,—may God send to us in that day some angel of His own, as He sent Abigail to David—an angel, though clothed in human flesh and blood, with a message of peace and wisdom. And if any such should speak to us words of peace and wisdom, soothing us and rebuking us at once, and appealing to those feelings in us which are really the most noble, just because they are the most gentle, then let us not turn away in pride, and wrap ourselves up in our own anger, but let us receive these words as the message of God—whether they come from the lips of a woman, or of a servant, or even of a little child, for if we resist them we surely resist God—who has also given to us His Holy Spirit for that very purpose, that we may hear His message when He speaks. It was the Spirit of God in David which made him feel that Abigail's message was divine. The Spirit of God, hidden for a while behind his dark passions, like the sun by clouds, shone out clear again, and filled all his soul with light, showing him his duty, and giving back peace and brightness to his mind.

God grant that whenever we are tried like David we may find that that Holy Spirit has not left us, but that even if a first storm of anger shall burst, it shall pass over quickly, and the day star arise in our hearts, and the Lord lift up the light of His countenance upon us, and give us peace.

XIV

DAVID'S LOYALTY

OR

TEMPTATION RESISTED

"So David and Abishai came to the people by night: and, behold, Saul lay sleeping within the trench, and his spear stuck in the ground at his bolster; but Abner and the people lay round about him. Then said Abishai to David, God hath delivered thine enemy into thine hand this day: now therefore let me smite him, I pray thee, with the spear even to the earth at once, and I will not smite him the second time. And David said to Abishai, Destroy him not: for who can stretch forth his hand against the Lord's anointed, and be guiltless? David said furthermore, As the Lord liveth, the Lord shall smite him; or his day shall come to die; or he shall descend into battle, and perish. The Lord forbid that I should stretch forth mine hand against the Lord's anointed; but, I pray thee, take thou now the spear that is at his bolster, and the cruise of water, and let us go."—1 Sam. xxvi. 7-11.

David stands for all times as the pattern of true loyalty—loyalty under the most extreme temptation. Knowing that he is to be king himself hereafter, he yet remains loyal to his king though unjustly persecuted to the death. Loyal he is to the end, because he has faith and obedience. Faith tells him that if king he is to be, king he will be, in God's good time. If God had promised, God will perform. He must not make himself king. He must not take the matter into his own hand. Obedience tells him that Saul is still his master, and he is bound to him. If Saul be a bad master, that does not give him leave to be a bad servant. The sacred bond still remains, and he must not break it. But Saul is more. He is king—the Lord's anointed, the general of the armies of the living God. His office is sacred; his person is sacred. He is a public personage, and David must not lift up his hand against him in a private quarrel.

Twice David's faith and obedience are tried fearfully. Twice

Saul is in his power. Twice the temptation to murder him comes before him. The first time David and his men are in one of the great branching caves of Engaddi, the desolate limestone cliffs, two thousand feet high, which overhang the Dead Sea—and Saul is hunting him, as he says, as a partridge on the mountains. "And it came to pass when Saul had returned from following the Philistines, that it was told him saying, Behold David is in the cave of Engedi. And Saul took three thousand chosen men out of all Israel, and went to seek David and his men upon the rocks of the wild goats. And he came to the sheepcotes, and by the way there was a cave; and Saul went in, and David and his men remained in the sides of the cave. And the men of David said unto him, Behold the day of which the Lord said unto thee, Behold I will deliver thine enemy into thy hand, and thou mayest do to him as seemeth good unto thee. Then David arose, and cut off the skirt of Saul's robe privily. And it came to pass afterwards, that David's heart smote him, because he had cut off Saul's skirt. And he said unto his men, The Lord forbid that I should do this thing unto my master, the Lord's anointed, to stretch forth mine hand against him, seeing he is the anointed of the Lord. So David stayed his servants." And afterwards Saul rose up, not knowing what had happened, and David followed him. And when Saul looked back, David stooped down with his face to the earth and bowed himself before Saul, and spoke many noble words to his king (1 Sam. xxiv. 1-8).

And David's nobleness has its reward. It brings out nobleness in return to Saul himself. It melts his heart for a time. "And it came to pass that when David had made an end of speaking, that Saul said, Is this thy voice, my son David? And Saul lifted up his voice, and wept. And he said to David, 'Thou art more righteous than I—for thou hast rewarded me good, whereas I have rewarded thee evil. And thou hast shewed me this day how thou hast dealt with me; for as much as when the Lord delivered me into thine hand, thou killedst me not. For if a man find his enemy, will he let him go well away? Wherefore the Lord reward thee good for that thou hast done unto me this day. And now, behold, I know well that thou shalt surely be king, and that the kingdom of Israel shall be established in thine hand.'"

And so it will be with you, my friends. "If thine enemy hunger, feed him; if he thirst, give him drink, for so thou shalt heap coals of fire on his head." Thou shalt melt the hardness of his heart. Thou shalt warm the coldness of his heart. Nobleness in thee shall bring out in answer nobleness in him, and if not, thou hast done thy duty, and the Lord judge between him and thee.

But Saul's repentance does not last. Soon after we find him

again hunting David in the wilderness, seemingly from mere caprice, and without any fresh cause of offence. The Ziphites—dwellers in the forests of the south of Judea—came to Saul and said, "Doth not David hide himself in the hill of Hachilah. Then Saul arose and went down to the wilderness, having three thousand chosen men of Israel with him, to seek David in the wilderness of Ziph. And Saul pitched in the hill of Hachilah. But David abode in the wilderness, and he saw that Saul came after him into the wilderness." Again Saul lies down to sleep—in an entrenched camp, and David and Abishai, his nephew, go down to the camp at night as spies. Then comes the story of my text—how Abishai would have slain Saul, and David forbade him to lift his hand against the Lord's anointed, and left Saul to the judgment of God, which he knew must come sooner or later—and merely took the spear from his bolster and the cruse of water to show he had been there.

Once again Saul's heart gives way at David's nobleness: for when David and Abishai got away while Saul and his guards all slept, David calls to Abner (verse 14-25), and rebukes him for not having guarded his king better. "Art not thou a valiant man? Wherefore, then, hast thou not kept thy lord the king? The thing is not good that thou hast done: As the Lord liveth, ye are worthy to die, because you have not kept your master, the Lord's anointed. And now see where the king's spear is, and the cruse of water that was at his bolster. And Saul knew David's voice, and said, Is this thy voice, my son David? And David said, It is my voice, my lord, O king. Wherefore does my lord then thus pursue after his servant? for what have I done? Now therefore, let not my blood fall to the earth, for the king of Israel is come out to seek a flea, as when one doth hunt a partridge. Then said Saul, I have sinned: return, my son David, for I will no more do thee harm, because my soul was precious in thine eyes. Behold, I have played the fool, and have erred exceedingly."

But David can trust him no longer. Weak, violent, and capricious, Saul's repentance is real for the time, but it does not last. He means what he says at the moment; but when some fresh base suspicion crosses his mind, his promises and his repentance are all forgotten. A terrible trial it is to David, to have his noble forgiveness and forbearance again and again bring forth no fruit—to have to do with a man whom he cannot trust. There are few sorer trials than that for living man. Few which tempt him more to throw away faith and patience, and say, "I cannot submit to this misconduct over and over again. It must end, and I will end it, by some desperate action, right or wrong."

And, in fact, it does seem as if David was very near yielding to temptation, the last and worst temptation which befalls men in his situation—to turn traitor and renegade, to go over to the enemies of his country and fight with them against Saul. That has happened too often to men in David's place; who have so ended a glorious career in shame and confusion. And we find that David does at last very nearly fall into it. It creeps on him, little by little, as it has on other men in his place, but it does creep on. He loses patience and hope. He says, I shall perish one day by the hand of Saul, and he goes down into the low country, to the Philistines, whose champion, Goliath, he had killed, and makes friends with them. And Achish, king of Gath, gives him a town called Ziklag, to live in, he and his men. From it he goes out and attacks the wild Arabs, the Amalekites. And then he tells lies to Achish, saying, that he has been attacking his own countrymen, the Jews. And by that lie he brings himself into a very great strait—as all men who tell lies are sure to do.

When Achish and his Philistines go next to fight against the Jews, Achish asks David and his men to go with him and his army. And then begins a very dark story. What David meant to do we are not told; but one thing is clear, that whatever he did, he must have disgraced himself for ever, if God had not had mercy on him. He is forced to go. For he can give no reason why he should not. So he goes; and in the rear with the Philistine king, in the post of honour, as his bodyguard. What is he to do? If he fights against his own people, he covers himself with eternal shame, and loses his chance of ever being king. If he turns against Achish and his Philistines in the battle he covers himself with eternal shame likewise, for they had helped him in his distress, and given him a home.

But God has mercy on him. The lords of the Philistines take offence at his being there, and say that he will play traitor to them in the battle (which was but too likely), and force king Achish to send him home to Ziklag, and so God delivers him out of the trap which he has set for himself, by lying.

But God punishes him on the spot. When he comes back to his town, it is burnt with fire, utterly desolate, a heap of blackened ruins, without a living soul therein. And now the end is coming, though David thinks not of it. He had committed his cause to God. He had said, when Saul lay sleeping at his feet, and Abishai would have smitten him through, "Who can stretch forth his hand against the Lord's anointed. As the Lord liveth, the Lord shall smite him, or he shall come to die, or he shall go down into battle and perish."

And on the third day a man—a heathen Amalekite—comes to Ziklag to David with his clothes rent, and earth upon his head.

Israel has been defeated in Mount Gilboa with a great slaughter. The people far and wide have fled from Hermon across the plain, and the Philistines have taken possession, cutting the land of Israel in two. And Saul and Jonathan, his son, are dead. The Amalekite has proof of it. There is the crown which was on Saul's head, and the bracelet that was on his arm. He has brought them to David to curry favour with him. Saul, he says, was wounded, and asked him to kill him (2 Sam. i. 6-10). It is a lie. Saul had killed himself, falling on his own sword, to escape torture and insult from the Philistines, and the Amalekite is caught in his own trap. Out of his own mouth will David judge him. How dare he stretch forth his hand against the Lord's anointed? Let one of the young men fall on him, and kill him. And so the wretch dies.

And then bursts forth all the nobleness of David's heart. He thinks of Saul no longer as the tyrant who has hunted him for years, who has put on him the last and worst insult of taking away his wife, and giving her to another man. He thinks of him only as his master, his king, the grand and terrible warrior, the terror of Ammonites, Amalekites, and Philistines, the deliverer of his country in many a bloody fight, and he bursts out into that fine old lamentation over Saul and Jonathan, sentences of which have been proverbs in the mouths of men to this day. "How are the mighty fallen! Tell it not in Gath, publish it not in the streets of Askelon; lest the daughters of the Philistines rejoice, lest the daughters of the uncircumcised triumph. Ye mountains of Gilboa, let there be no dew, neither let there be rain, upon you, nor fields of offerings: for there the shield of the mighty is vilely cast away, the shield of Saul, as though he had not been anointed with oil. From the blood of the slain, from the fat of the mighty, the bow of Jonathan turned not back, and the sword of Saul returned not empty. Saul and Jonathan were lovely and pleasant in their lives, and in their death they were not divided: they were swifter than eagles, they were stronger than lions. Ye daughters of Israel, weep over Saul, who clothed you in scarlet, with other delights, who put on ornaments of gold upon your apparel. How are the mighty fallen in the midst of the battle! O Jonathan, thou wast slain in thine high places. I am distressed for thee, my brother Jonathan: very pleasant hast thou been unto me: thy love to me was wonderful, passing the love of woman. How are the mighty fallen, and the weapons of war perished!" (2 Sam. i. 19-27).

Let each and every one of us, my friends, imitate David's loyalty, and be true to our duty, true to our masters, true to our country and true to our queen, through whatever trials and temptations. Above all, let us learn from David to obey; and remember that to obey we need not become cringing and slavish, or give up independence and high spirit. David did neither. Unless you learn to obey, as David did, you will never learn to rule. Imitate David—and so you will imitate David's greater son, even our Lord Jesus Christ. For herein David is a type of Christ.

One might say truly that David's spirit was in Christ—if the very opposite was not the fact, that the spirit of Christ was in David, even the spirit of loyalty and obedience, toward God and man. The spirit which made our Lord fulfil the whole law of Moses—though quite unnecessary, of course, for him—simply because He had chosen to be born a Jew, under Moses' law; the spirit which made Him obedient to the ordinance of the country in which He was born, made Him even pay tribute to Cæsar, the heathen conqueror, because the powers that ruled, were ordained of God. And yet that same spirit kept Him lofty and independent, high-minded and pure-minded. He could tell the people to observe and to do all that the scribes and Pharisees told them to do, because they sat in Moses' seat, and yet He could call those very scribes and Pharisees hypocrites, who made the law of no effect, and were bringing on themselves utter destruction.

That spirit, too, made Him loyal and obedient to God His Father in heaven. Doing not His own will, but the will of the Father who sent Him. Of Him it is written, that though He were a Son, yet learned He "obedience by the things which He suffered;" and that He received the perfect reward of perfect loyalty, because He had humbled and emptied Himself, and became obedient unto death even the death of the cross. Therefore God highly exalted Him, and gave Him a name which is above every name, that at the name of Jesus every knee should bow, of things in heaven, of things in the earth, and things under the earth, and every tongue confess that He is Lord and God, to the glory of God the Father.

This is a great mystery! How can we understand it? How can we understand the Divine and eternal bond between Father and Son? But this at least we can understand, that loyalty and obedience are Divine virtues, part of the likeness of Jesus Christ, the eternal Son of God, and therefore divine graces, the gift of God's holy Spirit.

May God pour out upon us that Spirit, as He poured it out on David, and make us loyal and obedient to our queen, and to all whom He has set over us; and loyal and obedient above all to Christ our heavenly king, and to God the Father, in whom we live, and move, and have our being.

XV

DAVID'S DEATH SONG

"And David spake unto the Lord the words of this song in the day that the Lord had delivered him out of the hand of all his enemies, and out of the hand of Saul: And he said, The Lord is my rock, and my fortress and my deliverer; the God of my rock; in him will I trust: he is my shield, and the horn of my salvation, my high tower, and my refuge, my saviour; thou savest me from violence."— 2 Sam. xxii. 1-3.

This is the death song of David; the last words of the great man—warrior, statesman, king, poet, prophet. A man of many joys and many sorrows, many virtues, and many crimes; but through them all, every inch a man. A man—heaped by God with every gift of body, and mind, and heart, and especially with strong and deep intense feeling. Right or wrong, he is never hard, never shallow, never light-minded. He is in earnest. Whatever happens to him, for good or evil, goes to his heart, and fills his whole soul, till it comes out again in song.

This it is which makes David the Psalmist. This it is which makes the Psalter a text book still for every soldier or sailor, for all men who have human hearts in them. This it is which will make his psalms live for ever. Because they are full of humanity, of the spirit of man, awakened and enlightened, and ennobled, by the Spirit of God.

Looking through these psalms of David, one is struck with astonishment at their variety. At what is called the versatility of his mind, that is, his ability to turn himself to every kind of subject, as it comes before him, and to sing of it—as man has never sung since. And one is the more astonished, when one remembers that many of the most beautiful of these Psalms must have been written while David was still a very young man. Though we have them, of course, only in a translation—though many of the words and phrases in them are difficult, sometimes impossible to understand, though they were written in a kind of verse which would give our English ears no pleasure, and were set to a music so utterly different from our own, that it would not sound like music to us. Yet, with all these disadvantages, they are beautiful as they stand, they sink into the ear, and into the heart, as what they are, the words of one inspired by God, who found beauty in every sight which he beheld, in every event which happened, even in every sorrow and every struggle in his own soul, and could sing of each and all of them in words and thoughts fresh from God, the fountain of all beauty and all truth.

But the peculiarity of David's psalms, after all, is from his intense faith in God. God is in all his thoughts. God is near him, guiding him, trying him, educating him, punishing him, sometimes he thinks for a moment, deserting him. But even then his mind is still full of God. It is God he wants, and the light of God's countenance, without which he cannot live, and leaving him in misery, and shame, and darkness, and out of the darkness he cries—My God, my God, why hast thou forsaken me? And, therefore, everything which happens to him shapes itself not into mere poetry, but into a prayer, or a hymn.

It is this which has made David for Christians now, as well as for Jews of old, the great master and teacher of heart religion. In the early church, in the middle ages, as now, Catholic alike and Protestant, whosoever has feared God and sought after righteousness; whosoever has known and sorrowed over the sinfulness and weakness of his own heart; whosoever has believed that the Lord God was dealing with him as with a son, educating him, chastening him, purifying him and teaching him, by the chances and changes of his mortal life; whosoever, I say, has had any real taste of vital experimental religion—to David's Psalms he has gone, as to a treasure house, to find there his own feelings, his own doubts, his own joys, his own thoughts of God and His providence—reflected as in a glass; everything which he would say, said for him already, in words which will never be equalled on earth.

There are psalms among them of bitter agony, cries as of a lost child, like that 6th psalm—"Oh Lord, rebuke me not in Thine anger, neither chasten me in Thy hot displeasure," &c. And yet ending like that, with a sudden flash of faith, and hope, and joy, which is a peculiar mark of David's character, faith in God triumphing over all the chances and changes of mortal life. "The Lord hath heard the voice of my weeping. The Lord will receive my prayer, all mine enemies shall be confounded and sore vexed. They shall be turned back and put to shame."

There are psalms again which are prayers for guidance and teaching like the 5th Psalm—"Lead me, O Lord, in thy righteousness because of mine enemies: make thy way plain before my face."

There are psalms, again, of Natural Religion, such as the 8th and the 19th and the 29th, the words of a man who had watched and studied nature by day and night, as he kept his sheep upon the mountains, and wandered in the desert with his men. "I will consider thy heavens, the works of thy hand, the moon and the stars which thou hast ordained... the fowls of the air and the fishes of the sea"... (Ps. viii. 3-8). "The heavens declare the glory of God: and the firmament sheweth his handi-work" (Ps. xix. 1-6). "It is the Lord that commandeth the water: it is the glorious God that maketh the thunder: it is the Lord that ruleth the sea: the voice of the Lord breaketh the cedar trees: the voice of the Lord divideth the flames of fire: the voice of the Lord shaketh the wilderness: the Lord sitteth above the water flood," &c. (Ps. xxix.).

There are psalms of deep religious experience like the 32d.—"Blessed is he whose unrighteousness is forgiven, and whose sin is covered ... Thou art a place to hide me in.... Thy hand is heavy upon me day and night... I will acknowledge my sin unto Thee."

There are psalms, and these are almost the most important of all, such as the 9th, the 24th and 36th Psalms, which declare the providence and the kingdom of the Living God, with that great and prophetic 2d Psalm (ver. 1-5): "Why do the heathen so furiously rage together, and the people imagine vain things. The kings of the earth stand up, and the rulers take counsel together against the Lord, and against his anointed," &c.

There are psalms of deep repentance, of the broken and the contrite heart, like that famous 51st Psalm, which is used in all Christian churches to this day, as the expression of all true repentance, and which, even in our translation, by its awful simplicity, its slow sadness, expresses in its very sound the utterly crushed and broken heart. "Have mercy upon me, O God, after thy great goodness, according to the multitude of thy mercies do away mine offences.... Behold, I was shapen in iniquity, and in sin did my mother conceive.... The sacrifice of God is a troubled spirit, a broken and a contrite heart, O God, thou wilt not despise...." Then there are psalms, like the 26th, of a manful and stately confidence. The words of one who is determined to do right, who feels that on the whole he is doing it, and is not ashamed to say so. "Be thou my judge, for I have walked innocently.... Examine and prove me: try out my reins and my heart. I have not dwelt with vain persons, neither will I have fellowship with the deceitful.... I have hated the congregation of the wicked. I have loved the habitation of thy house." There are political psalms, full of weighty advice, to his sons after him, like the 115th Psalm.

There are psalms of the most exquisite tenderness, like the 23d Psalm, written perhaps while he himself was still a shepherd boy, and he looked upon his flocks feeding on the downs of Bethlehem, and sang, "The Lord is my shepherd, I shall not want," &c. And lastly, though I should not say lastly, for the variety of this wonderful man's psalms is past counting, there are psalms of triumph and thanksgiving, which are miracles of beauty and grandeur. Take, for instance, the 34th, one of the earliest, when David was not more than twenty-five years old, when Abimelech drove him away, and he departed and sang, "I will bless the Lord at all times.... My soul shall make her boast in the Lord.... I sought the Lord, and he heard me, and delivered me out of all my fear. Lo the poor man crieth and the Lord heareth him.... The angel of the Lord tarrieth round about them that fear him, and delivereth them." And, as the grandest of all, as, indeed, it was meant to be, that wonderful 18th Psalm which David, the servant of the Lord, spake to the Lord in the day when the Lord delivered him out of the hand of all his enemies. "I will love thee, O Lord, my strength. The Lord is my strong rock and defence: my Saviour, my God, and my might, in whom I will trust, my buckler, the horn also of my salvation, and my refuge." This is, indeed, David's masterpiece. The only one which comes near it is the 144th. The loftiest piece of poetry, taken as mere poetry, though it is more, much more, in the whole world. Even in our translation, it rushes on with a force and a swiftness, which are indeed divine. Thought follows thought, image image, verse verse, before the breath of the Spirit of God, as wave leaps after wave before a mighty wind. Even now, to read that psalm rightly, should stir the heart like a trumpet. What must it have been like when sung by David himself? No wonder that those brave old Jews hung upon the lips of their warrior-poet and felt that the man who could sing to them of such thoughts, and not only sing them, but feel them likewise, was indeed a king and a prophet sent to them by God. A prophet, I say. They loved his songs not merely on account of the beauty of their poetry. Indeed, one hardly likes to talk of David's psalms as beautiful poetry. It seems unfair to them. For though they are beautiful poetry, they are far more, they are prophecy and preaching concerning God. They preach and declare to the Jews the Living God. They are the speech of a man whose thoughts and works were begun, continued, and ended in God. A man who knew that God was about his path, and about his bed, and spying out all his ways. A man whose one fixed idea was, that God was leading and guiding him through life. That idea, "The Lord leads me," is the key-note of David's psalms, and makes them what they are, an inspired revelation of Almighty God.

But is that idea true? Of course, you answer, it is true, because it is in the Bible. But that is not the question. That is rather putting the question aside, which is, Do we believe it to be true, and find it to be true? We believe that God was leading David because we read it in the Bible. But do we believe that God is leading us? If not, what is the use of our reading David's psalms, either in private or publicly in church every Sunday? You all know how largely we use them, but why? If we are not in the same case as David was, what right have we to take David's words into our mouths? We do not fancy that there is any magical virtue in repeating the same words, as foolish people used to repeat charms and spells. Our only right, our only excuse for saying or singing David's psalms in public or in private, must be, that as David was, so are we in this world, under the continual guidance of God.

And therefore it is that the Church bids us to use these psalms in our devotions, day by day, all the year round—that we may know that our God is David's God, our temptations David's temptations, our fears David's fears, our hopes David's hopes, our struggles and triumphs over what is wrong in our hearts and in the world around us, are the same as David's. That we are not to fancy, because David was an inspired prophet, that therefore he was in a different case from us, of different passions from ours, or that his words are too sacred and holy for us to use. Not so, we are to believe the very contrary. We are to believe that no prophecy of Scripture is of any private interpretation—that is—has not merely to do with the man who spoke it first—but that because David spoke by the Spirit of God, who is no respecter of persons, therefore his words apply to you, and to me, and to every human being—that David is revealing to us the everlasting laws of God's Spirit, and of God's providence, whereby He works alike in every Christian soul, and then, therefore, whatever our sin may be, whatever our sorrows may be, whatever our station in life may be, we have a right to offer up to God our repentance, our doubts, our fears, our hopes, our thanksgivings, in the very words which David used two thousand years and more ago, certain that they are the right words, better words than we can find for ourselves, exactly fitting our own souls, and fitting too the mind and will of Almighty God, because they are inspired by the same Spirit of God who descended on us, when we were baptized unto Christ's Church.

And for that, my friends, we have an example—as we have for everything else—in our Lord Jesus Christ Himself. For He, in the hour of His darkest agony, when He hung upon the cross for our sins, and the sin of all mankind, and when (worse than all other agony, or shame), there came over Him the deepest horror of all—the feeling, but for a moment, that God had forsaken Him—even then, He who spake as never man spake, did not disdain to use the words of David, and cry, in the opening verse of that 22d psalm, every line of which applies so strangely to Him himself, "My God, my God, why hast Thou forsaken me?" So did our Lord bequeath, as it were, with His dying breath, to all Christians for ever, as the fit and true expression of all that they should ever experience, the psalms of His great earthly ancestor, David, the sweet singer of Israel.

My friends, neglect not that precious bequest of your dying Lord. Read those psalms, study them, tune your hearts and minds to them more and more; and you will find in them an inexhaustible treasury of wisdom, and comfort, and of the knowledge of God, wherein standeth your eternal life.

XVI

AHAB AND MICAIAH—THE CHRISTIAN DEAD ALIVE FOE EVERMORE

"And the King of Israel said to Jehosaphat, There is yet one man, Micaiah the son of Imlah, by whom we may enquire of the Lord: but I hate him; for he doth not prophesy good concerning me, but evil."...—1 Kings xxii.8.

If you read the story of Micaiah the Prophet, and King Ahab in the 22d chapter of the 1st Book of Kings, you will, I think, agree that Ahab showed himself as foolish as he was wicked. He hated Micaiah for telling him the truth. And when he heard the truth and was warned of his coming end, he went stupidly to meet it, and died as the fool dies. Foolishness and wickedness often go hand in hand. Certainly they did in that miserable king's case.

But now, my friends, while we find fault with wretched Ahab, let us take care that we are not finding fault with ourselves also. If we do what Ahab did, we have no right to despise him for doing what we do. With what judgment we judge we shall be judged, and the same measure which we measure out to Ahab, God will measure out to us. All these things are written for our example, that we may see our faults in other men, as in a glass, and seeing how ugly sin and folly is, and to what misery it leads, may learn to avoid it, and look at home, and see that we are not treading the same path. Else what use in reading these stories of good men and bad men of old times? The very use of them is to make us remember that they were men of like passions with ourselves, and learn from their example; as we may do easily enough from that of Ahab.

"There remaineth yet one prophet—but I hate him." How often have we said that in our hearts! Do you think not? Let me show you then.

How often when we are in trouble or anxiety do we go everywhere to get comfort, before we go to God's word? When a young lad falls into wild ways, and gets into trouble by his own folly, then to whom does he go for comfort? Too often, to other wild lads like himself, or to foolish and wicked women, who will flatter him, and try to make him easy in his sins, and say to him as the false prophets said to Ahab, "Go on and prosper—why be afraid? Why should you not enjoy yourself? Never mind what your father and mother say, never mind what the parson says. You will do well enough. All will come right somehow. Come and drink, and drive away sorrow."

And all the while the poor lad gets no comfort from these false friends. He likes to listen to them, because they flatter him up in his sins; but all the while his heart is heavy. Like Ahab, he has a secret fear that all will not come right; he feels that he will not do well enough; and he knows that there remaineth yet a prophet of the Lord, who will not prophesy good of him but evil—and that is the Bible, and the prayer-book, and the sermon he hears at church—and therefore he hates them. And so, many a time he will not go to church for fear of hearing there that he is wrong, perhaps something in the sermon, which hits him hard, and makes him ashamed of himself, and angry with the preacher. So for fear of hearing the truth, and having his sins set before his face, he stays away from church, and passes his Sundays like a heathen, because he has no mind to repent and mend, and be a good Christian.

Foolish fellow! As if he could escape God's judgment by shutting his ears to it. As well try to stop the thunder from rolling in the sky, by stopping his ears to that! The thunder is there, whether he choose to hear it or not. And whether he comes to church or not, God's law stands sure, that the wages of sin is death. Does the man fancy that God's law is shut up within the church walls, and that so he can keep clear of it by staying away from church? My friends, God's law is over the whole country, and over every cottage and field in it—about our path and about our bed, and spying out all our ways. The darkness is no darkness to God. God's judgments are in all the earth; and whether or not we choose to find them out, they will find us out just the same, as they found out Ahab, when his cup was full, and his time was come.

How many a poor lad, too, who has got into trouble, thinks he shall escape God's judgments by going across the sea; but he finds himself mistaken! He finds that the wages of sin are misery and shame and ruin, in Australia just as much as in England, and that all the gold in the diggings cannot redeem his soul, or prevent his being an unhappy self-condemned man if he does wrong.

How many a poor lad, too, who has got into trouble, has fancied that he could escape God's judgments by going for a soldier, and has found out that he too was mistaken! Perhaps God's judgment has found him out, as it found out Ahab, on the field of battle, and a chance shot has taught him, as it taught Ahab, that there is no hiding-place from the Lord who made him. Or perhaps God's judgments have come in fever, and hunger, and cold, and weariness, and miserable lonely labour; and with that hunger of body has come a hunger of his soul—a hunger after the bread of life, and the word of God! Ah! how many a poor fellow in his pain and misery has longed for the crumbs which used to fall from God's table, when he was a boy at home! for a word of good advice, though it were never so sharp and plain spoken—or a lesson such as he used to hear at school, or a tract, or a bit of a book, or anybody or anything which will put his poor wandering soul in the right way. He used to hate such things when he was at home, because they warned him of his bad ways; but now he feels a strange longing for that very good talk which he hated once, and so like David of old, out of the deep he cries unto the Lord. And when that cry comes up out of a sinful conscience-stricken, self-condemned heart, be sure it does not come up in vain. The Lord hears it, and the Lord answers it. Yes, I know it for certain; for many a sad and yet pleasant story I have heard, how brave men who went out from England, full of strength and health, and full of sin and folly too,—and there in that blood-stained Crimea, when their strength and their health had faded, and there was nothing round them or before them but wounds, and misery, and death; how there at last they found Christ, or rather were found by Him, and opened their eyes at last to see God's judgments for their sins, and confessed their own sin and God's justice, and received His precious promises of pardon, even in the agonies of death; and found amid the rage and noise of war, the peace of God, which this world's pleasures never gave them, and which this world's wounds, and fever, and battle, and sudden death cannot take away.

And after that, it matters little for a man what happens to him. For if he lives, he lives unto the Lord; and if he dies, he dies unto the Lord. He may come home, well and strong, once more to do his duty, where God has put him, a sadder man perhaps, but at least a soberer and a wiser man, who has learnt to endure hardship, not merely as a soldier of the Queen, but as a good soldier of Jesus Christ too, ready to fight against sin and wrong-doing in himself and in his neighbours.

Or he may come home a cripple, to be honoured and to be kept too (as he deserves to be) at his country's expense. But if he be a wise man he will not regret even the loss of a limb. That is a cheap price to pay for having gained what is worth all the limbs in a man's body, a clear conscience and a right life. "If thy hand offend thee cut it off." Better to enter into life halt and maimed, as many a gallant man has done in war time, than having two hands and two feet to be cast out.

Or perhaps his grave is left behind there, upon those lonely Crimean downs, and his comrades are returning without him, and all whom he knew, and all whom he loved, are looking for him at home. There his grave is, and must be; and "the foe and the stranger will tread on his head, and they far away on the billow."

But at least he has not died like Ahab—a shameful and pitiable death. He has done his work and conquered. He has died like a man, whom men honour. Even so it is well. And if he have died in the Lord, a penitent Christian man, he is not dead at all. He does not lie in that grave in a foreign land. All of him that strangers' feet can tread upon is but what we called his body; and yet which was not even his body, but the mere husk and shell of him, the flesh and bones with which his body was clothed in this life; while he, he himself, is nearer God than ever, and nearer, too, than ever to his comrades who seem to have left him, and to the parents and the friends who are weeping for him at home. Ay, nearer to them, more able, I firmly believe, to help and comfort them, now that he is alive for ever, in the heaven of God, than he would if he were only alive here on the earth of God—more able perhaps to help them now by his prayers than he ever would have been by the labour of his hands. Be that as it may, Blessed are the dead who die in the Lord, for they rest from their labours, and their works do follow them. A fearful labour is the soldier's, and an ugly work; and he has done it; and doubt not it has followed him, and is recorded for him in the book of God for ever!

XVII

WHAT IS CHANCE?

"By one man sin entered into the world, and death by sin; and so death passed upon all men, because all have sinned."—Romans v. 12.

All death is a solemn and fearful thing. When it comes to an old person, one cannot help feeling it often a release, and saying, "He has done his work—he has sorrowed out his sorrows, he has struggled his last struggle, and wept his last tear: let him go to his rest and be peaceful at last."

But when death comes suddenly to people in the prime of life, who but yesterday were as busy and as lively as any of us, and we are face to face with death, and see the same face we knew in life—not wasted, not worn, young and lusty as ever, seemingly asleep,—something at our heart as well as in our eyes, tells us that there is more than sleep in that strange, sharp, quiet smile—and we know in spite of ourselves that the man is dead. And then strange questions rise in us, "Is that he whom we knew? that still piece of clay, waiting only a few days before it returns to its dust? It is the face of him, the shape of him, it is what we knew him by. It is the very same body of which when we met it on the road we said, "He is coming." And yet is it he? Where is he himself? Can he hear us? Can he see us? Does he remember us as we remember him? Surely he must. He cannot be gone away—there he lies still on that bed before us!"

And then we are ready to say to ourselves, "It must be a mistake, a dream. He cannot be dead. He will wake. We shall meet him to-morrow in his old place, about his old work. He dead? Impossible! Impossible to believe that we shall never see him again—never any more till we too die!"

And then when such thoughts come over us, we cannot help going on to say, "What is this death? this horrible thing which takes husbands from their wives, and children from their parents, and those who love from those who love them? What is it? How came this same death loose in the world? What right has it here, under the bright sun, among the pleasant fields, this cruel, pitiless death, destroying God's handi-work, God's likeness, just as it is growing to its prime of beauty and usefulness?"

And then—there—by the bedside of the young at least, we do feel that death must be God's enemy—that it is a hateful, cruel, evil thing—accursed in the sight of a loving, life-giving God, as much as it is hated by poor mortal man.

And then, we feel, there must be something wrong between man and God. Man must be fallen and corrupt, must be out of his right place and state in some way or other, or this horrible death would not have got power over us! What right has death in the world, if man has not sinned or fallen?

And then we cannot help going further and saying, "This cruel death! it may come to me, young, strong, and healthy as I am. It may come to-morrow; it may come this minute; it may come by a hundred diseases, by a hundred accidents, which I cannot foresee or escape, and carry me off to-morrow, away from all I know and all I love, and all I like to see and to do. And where would it take me to, if it did take me? What should I be? What should I see? What should I know, after they had put this body of mine into that narrow house in the church-yard, and covered it out of sight till the judgment day?" Oh, my friends, what a thought for you, and me, and every human being! We might die to-night, even as those whom we know of died!

But perhaps some of you young people are saying to yourselves, "You are trying to frighten us, but you shall not frighten us. We know very well that it is not a common thing for a young person to die—not one in a hundred (except in a war time) dies in the prime of his years; and therefore the chances are that we shall not die young either. The chances are that we shall live to be old men and women, and we are not going to be frightened about dying forty years before our death. So in the meanwhile we will go our own way and enjoy ourselves. It will be time enough to think of death when death draws near."

Well then, if you have these thoughts, I will ask you, what do you mean by chance? You say, the chances are against your dying young. Pray what are these wonderful things called chances, which are to keep you alive for thirty or forty or fifty years more? Did you ever hear a chance, or see a chance? Or did you ever meet with any one who had? Did any one ever see a great angel called Chance flying about keeping people from dying? What is chance on which you depend as you say for your life? What is chance which you fancy so much stronger than God? For as long as the chance is against your dying, you are not afraid of neglecting God and disobeying God, and therefore you must suppose that chance is stronger than God, and quite able to keep God's anger off from you for thirty or forty years, till you choose to repent and amend. What sort of thing is this wonderful chance, which is going to keep you alive?

Perhaps you will say, "All we meant when we said that the chances were against our dying was that God's will was against our dying."

Did you only mean that? Then why put the thought of God away by foolish words about chance? For you know that it is God and God only who keeps you alive. You must look at that, you must face that. If you are alive now, God keeps you so. If you live forty years more, God will make you live that time. And He who can make you live, can also let you not live; and then you will die. God can withdraw the breath of life from you or me or any one at any moment. And then where would our chances of not dying be? We should die here and now, and know that God is the Lord and not chance...

But think again. If God makes you alive He must have some reason for making you alive. For mind—it is not as you fancy, that when God leaves you alone you live, and when He puts forth His power and visits you, you die. Not that, but the very opposite. For in Adam all die. Our bodies are dead by reason of sin, and in the midst of life we are in death. There is a seed of death in you and me and every little child. While we are eating and drinking and going about our business, fancying that we cannot help living, we carry the seeds of disease in our own bodies, which will surely kill us some day, even if we are not cut off before by some sudden accident. That is true, physicians know that it is true. Our bodies carry in them from the very cradle the seeds of death; and therefore it is not because God leaves us alone that we live. We live because God, our merciful heavenly Father, does not leave us alone, but keeps down those seeds of disease and death by His Spirit, who is the Lord and Giver of Life.

God's Spirit of Life is fighting against death in our bodies from the moment we are born. And then, as Moses says, when He withdraws that Spirit of His, then it is that we die and are turned again to our dust. So that our living a long time or a short time, does not depend on Chance, or on our own health or constitution, but entirely on how long God may choose to keep down the death which is lying in us, ready to kill us at any moment, and certain to kill us sooner or later.

And yet people fancy that they live because they cannot help living, unless God interferes with them and makes them die. They fancy, thoughtless and ignorant as they are, that when they are in health, God leaves them alone, and that therefore when they are in health they may leave God alone.

My friends, I tell you that it is God, and not our constitution or chance either which keeps you alive; as you will surely find out the moment after the last breath has left your body. And therefore I ask you solemnly the plain question, "For what does God keep you alive?" For what? Will a man keep plants in his garden which bear neither fruit nor flowers? Will a man keep stock on his farm which will only eat and never make profit; or a servant in his house who will not work? Much more, will a man keep a servant who will not only be idle himself, but quarrel with his fellow servants, lead them into sin and shame, and teach them to disobey their master? What man in his senses would keep such plants, such stock, such servants? And yet God keeps hundreds and thousands in His garden and in His house for years and years, while they are doing no good to Him, and doing harm to those around them.

How many are there who never yet did one thing to make their companions better, and yet have done many a thing to make their companions worse! Then why are they alive still? Why does not God rid Himself of them at once and let them die, instead of cumbering the ground? I know but one reason. If they were only God's plants, or His stock, or His servants, He might rid Himself of them. But they are something far nearer and dearer to Him than that. They are His children, and therefore He has mercy on them. They are redeemed by the blood of the Lord Jesus Christ, the Lamb slain before the foundation of the world; and therefore for the sake of the Lord Jesus Christ, God looks on them with long-suffering and tender loving-kindness. Man was made in God's likeness at first, and was the son of God. And therefore howsoever fallen and corrupt man's nature is now, yet God loves him still, even though he be a heathen or an infidel. How much more for you, my friends, who know that you are God's children, who have been declared to be His children by Holy Baptism, and grafted into Christ's church. You at least are bound to believe that God preserves you from death, because He loves you. He protects you every day and every hour, as a father takes care of His children, and keeps them out of dangers which they cannot see or understand.

Yes! this is plain truth—your heavenly Father is keeping you alive! Oh, do not make that truth an excuse for forgetting and disobeying your heavenly Father!

Why does He keep you alive? Surely because He expects something of you. And what does He expect of you? What does any good father expect of his children? Why does he help and protect them? Not from mere brute instinct, as beasts take care of their young when they are little, and then as soon as they are grown up cast them off and forget them. No. He takes care of his children because he wishes them to grow up like himself, to be a comfort and a help and a pride to him.

And God takes care of you and keeps you from death, for the very same reason. God desires that you should grow up like Himself, godly and pure, leading lives like His Son Jesus Christ. God desires that you should grow up to the stature of perfect men and women, which is the likeness of Jesus Christ your Lord.

But if you turn God's grace in keeping you alive into a cloak for licentiousness and an excuse for sinning—if, when God keeps you alive that you may lead good lives, you take advantage of His fatherly love to lead bad lives—if you go on returning God evil for good, and ungratefully and basely presume on His patience and love to do the things which He hates, what must you expect? God loves you, and you make that an excuse for not loving Him; God does everything for you, and you make that an excuse for doing nothing for God; God gives you health and strength, and you make that an excuse for using your health and strength just in the way He has forbidden. What can be more ungrateful? What can be more foolish? Oh, my friends, if one of our children behaved to us in return for our care and love a hundredth part as shamefully as most of us behave to God our Father, what should we think of them? What should we say of them?

Oh, beware, beware! God is a righteous God, strong and patient, and God is provoked every day, and bears it according to His boundless love and patience. But "if a man will not turn," says the same text, "He will whet His sword." And then—woe to the careless and ungrateful sinner. God will cut him down and bring him low. God will take from him his health, or his money, or his blind peace of mind; and by affliction after affliction, and shame after shame, and disappointment after disappointment, teach him that his youth, and his health, and his money, and all that he has, are his Father's gifts and not his own property—and that His Father will take them away from him, till he feels his own weakness, till he sees that he is really not his own but God's property, body and soul, and goes back to his heavenly Father and cries, "Father, I have sinned against heaven and before Thee, and am no more worthy to be called Thy son. I have taken Thy gifts and gone away with them from Thy house unto the far country of sin, and wasted them in riotous living, till I have had to fill my belly with the husks which the swine did eat. I have had no profit out of all my sins, of which I am now ashamed. I have robbed Thee and abused Thy gifts and

Thy love. Father, take me back, for I have sinned, and am not worthy to be called Thy child."

XVIII

EARTHLY AND HEAVENLY WISDOM

OR

STOOP TO CONQUER

"The Lord by wisdom hath founded the earth; by understanding hath he established the heavens."— Prov. iii. 19.

Did it ever strike you as a very remarkable and important thing, that after saying in Proverbs iii. that Wisdom is this precious treasure, and bidding his son seek for her because (verse 16) "Length of days is in her right hand, and in her left hand riches and honour: Her ways are ways of pleasantness, and all her paths are peace,"—Solomon goes on immediately to say (verses 19, 20), "The Lord by Wisdom hath founded the earth, and established the heavens?"

By Wisdom: by the very same Wisdom, Solomon says, which is to give men length of days, and riches, and honour. Is not this curious at least? That there is but one wisdom for God and man? That man's true wisdom is a pattern of God's wisdom? That a man to prosper in the world must get the very same wisdom by which God made and rules the world? Curious. But most blessed news, my friends, if we will think over what it means. I will try to explain it to you: first, as to this world which we see; next, as to the heavenly world of spirits which we do not see.

You have, many of you, heard the word "Science." Many of you of course know what it means. That it means wisdom and learning about this earth and all things in it. Many more of you of course know that in the last hundred years science has improved in a most wonderful way, and is improving every day; that we have now gas-lights, steam-engines, cotton-mills, railroads, electric telegraphs, iron ships, and a hundred curious and useful machines and manufactures of which our great-grandfathers never dreamed; that our knowledge of different countries, of medicines, of the laws of health and disease, and of all in short which has to do with man's bodily life, is increasing day by day; and that all these discoveries are very great blessings; they give employment and food to millions who would otherwise have had nothing to do; they bring vast wealth into this country, and all the countries which trade with us. They enable this land of England to support four times as many human beings as it did two hundred years ago; they make many of the necessaries of life cheaper, so that in many cases a poor man may now have comforts which his grandfather never heard of.

I know that there is a dark side to this picture; that with all this increase of wisdom, there has come conceit, and trust in deceitful riches, and want of trust in God, and obedience to His law. I know that in some things we are not better, but worse than our forefathers; God forgive us for it! But the good came from God; and that man is very unwise and unthankful too, who despises God's great gift of science, because fallen man has defiled His gift as it passed through his unclean hands.

Look only at this one thing, as I said just now, that by all these wonderful discoveries and improvements, England is able to support four times as many Englishmen as it used of old, and that, if we feared God, and sought His kingdom better, I believe, England would support many more people yet—and see if that be not a thing to thank Almighty God for every day of our lives.

Now how did this wonderful change and improvement take place—suddenly, and, as it were, in the course of the last hundred years? Simply by mankind understanding the text (Prov. iii. 19), and by obeying it. I tell you a real truth, my friends, and it happened thus.

For more than sixteen hundred years after our Lord's time, mankind seem to have become hardly any wiser about earthly things, nay, even to have gone back. The land was no better tilled; goods were no more easily made; diseases were no better cured, than they had been sixteen hundred years before. And if any learned men longed to become very wise and cunning, and to get power over this world and the things in it, they flew off to witchcraft, charms, and magic, deceived by the devil's old lie, that the kingdom and the power and the glory of this world belonged to him and not to God.

But about two hundred and fifty years ago, it pleased God to open the eyes of one of the wisest men who ever lived, who was called Francis Bacon, Lord Verulam, Lord Chancellor of England, and to show him the real and right way of learning by which men can fulfil God's command to replenish the earth and subdue it. And Francis Bacon told all the learned men boldly that they had all been wrong together, and that their wisdom was no better than a sort of madness, as it is written, "The wisdom of man is foolishness with

God;" that the only way for man to be wise was to get God's wisdom, the wisdom with which He had founded the earth, and find out God's laws by which He had made this world.

"And then," he said, "if you can do that, you will be able to imitate God in your own small way. If you learn the laws by which God made all things, you will be able to invent new things for yourselves. For you can only subdue nature by obeying her." That was one of his greatest sayings, and by it he meant, that you can only subdue a thing and make it useful to you, by finding out the rules by which God made that thing, and by obeying them.

For instance, you cannot subdue and till a barren field, and make it useful, without knowing and obeying the laws and rules of that soil; and then you can subdue and conquer that field, and change and train it, as I may say, to grow what you like. You cannot conquer diseases without knowing and obeying the laws by which God has made man's body, and the laws by which fever and cholera and other plagues come.

Let me give you another instance. You all have seen lightning conductors, which prevent tall chimneys and steeples from being struck by storms, so that the lightning runs harmless downward. Now we can all see how this is conquering the force of lightning in a wonderful and beautiful way. But before you can conquer the lightning by a conductor, you must obey the lightning and its laws most carefully. If you make the conductor out of your own head and fancy, it will be of no use. You must observe and follow humbly the laws which God has given to the lightning. You must make the conductor of metal wire, or it will be useless. You must make it run through glazed rings, or it will be only more dangerous than no conductor at all; for God who made the lightning chose that it should be so, and you must obey if you wish to conquer.

Man could not conquer steam, and make it drive his engines and carry his ships across the seas, till he found out and obeyed the laws which God had given to steam; and so without breaking the laws, man turned them to his own use, and set the force of steam to turn his machines, instead of rushing idly out into the empty air.

So it is with all things, whether in heaven or earth. If you want to rule, you must obey. If you want to rise to be a master, you must stoop to be a servant. If you want to be master of anything in earth or heaven, you must, as that great Lord Verulam used to say, obey God's will revealed in that thing; and the man who will go his own way, and follow his own fancy, will understand nothing, and master nothing, and get comfort out of nothing in earth or heaven.

Well—when Lord Verulam told men his new wisdom, they laughed and scoffed, as fools always will at anything new. But one by one, wise men tried his plan, and found him right, and went on; and from that time those who followed Lord Verulam began discovering wonders of which they had never dreamed, and those who did not, but kept to the old way of witchcraft and magic, found out nothing, and made themselves a laughing stock. And after a while witchcraft vanished out of all civilised countries, and in its place came all the wonderful comforts and discoveries which we have now, and which under God, we owe to the wisdom of the great Lord Verulam. Cotton mills, steam engines, railroads, electric telegraphs, sanitary reforms, cheap books, penny postage, good medicine and surgery, and a thousand blessings more. That great Lord Chancellor has been the father of them all.

And a noble thought it is for us Church people, and a glorious testimony to the good training which the Church of England gives, that the three men, who more than any others laid the foundation of all our wonderful discoveries, I mean Lord Verulam, Mr. Boyle, and Sir Isaac Newton, were all of them heart and soul members of the Church of England.

I said just now that the man who will not obey, will never rule; that the man who will not stoop to be a servant, will never rise to be a master; that the man who neglects God's will and mind about things, and will follow his own will and fancy, will understand nothing, and master nothing, and get comfort out of nothing, either in earth or heaven.

Either in earth or heaven, I say. For the same rule which holds good in this earthly world, which we do see, holds good in the heavenly world which we do not see. Solomon does not part the two worlds, and I cannot. Solomon says the same rules which hold good about men's bodies, hold good about their souls. The great Lord Verulam used always to say the same, and we must believe the same. For see, Solomon says, that this same wisdom by which God made the worlds, will help our souls as well as our bodies; that it is not merely the earthly wisdom which brings a man length of life and riches, but heavenly wisdom, which is a tree of life to every one who lays hold of her (Prov. iii. 18). The heavenly wisdom which begins in trusting in the Lord with all our heart, the heavenly wisdom which is learnt by chastenings and afflictions, and teaches us that we are the sons of God, is the very same wisdom by which God founded the earth, and makes the clouds drop down dew! Strange at first sight; but not strange if we remember the Athanasian creed, and believe that God is one God, who has no parts or passions, and therefore cannot change or be divided.

Yes, my friends, God's wisdom is one—unchangeable, everlasting, and always like itself; and by the same wisdom by which

He made the earth and the heavens, by the same wisdom by which He made our bodies, has He made our souls; and therefore we can, and are bound to, glorify Him alike in our bodies and our spirits, for both are His.

It may not seem easy to understand this; but I will explain what I mean by an example. I just told you, that in earthly matters we must stoop to conquer; we must obey the laws which God has given to anything, before we can master and use that thing. And in matters about our own soul—about our behaviour to God—about our behaviour to our fellow-men, believe me there is no rule like the golden one of Lord Verulam's—stoop to conquer—obey if you wish to rule. For see now. What is there more common than this? It happens to each of us every day. We meet a fellow-man our equal, neither better nor worse than ourselves, and we want to make him do something. Now there are two ways in which we may set about that. We may drive our man, or we may lead him. You know well enough which of those two ways is likely to succeed best. If you try to drive the man, you say to yourself, "I know I am right. I see the thing in this light, and he is a fool if he does not see it in the same light. I choose to have the thing done, and done it shall be, and if he is stupid enough not to take my view of it, I will let him know who I am, and we will see which of us is the stronger!" So says many a man in his heart. But what comes of it? Nothing. For the other man gets angry, and determines to have his way in his turn. There is a quarrel and a great deal of noise; and most probably the thing is not done. Instead of the man getting what he wants, he has a fresh quarrel on his hands, and nothing more. So his blustering is no sign that he is really strong. For the strong man is the man who can get what he wants done. Is he not? Surely we shall all agree to that. And the proud, hot, positive, dictatorial, self-willed man is just the man, in a free country like this, who does not get what he wants done. He will not stoop—therefore he will not conquer.

But suppose we take another plan. Suppose instead of trying to drive, we try to lead. Suppose if we want a man to do anything, we begin by obeying him, and serving him, that we may afterwards lead him, and afterwards make use of him. There is a base, mean way of doing that, by flattering, and fawning, and cringing, which are certainly the devil's works. For the devil can put on the form of an angel of light; but we need not do that. We may serve and obey a man honestly and honourably, in order to get him to do what he ought to do. I will tell you what I mean.

Suppose when we have dealings with any man, we begin with him, as I was saying we ought to begin with earthly things—with a field for instance—we should say, before I begin to make this field bear the crop I want I must look it through and understand it. I must see what state it is in—what its soil is—what has been taken off it already—what the weather is—what state of drainage it is in, and so forth; and I must obey the rules of all these things, or my crop will come to nothing. So with this man. First of all, before I get anything out of the man, I must understand the man. I must find out what sort of temper and character he has, what his opinions are, how he has been brought up, how he has been accustomed to look at things—so as to be able to make allowance for all, else I shall never be able to understand how he looks at this one matter, or to make him understand my way of looking at it. And to do that—to understand the man, or make him understand me, I must begin by making a friend of him.

There, my friends—there is one of the blessed laws of the kingdom of Heaven, that in a free country (as this, thank God, is) the only sure way to get power and influence over people, is by making friends of them, by behaving like Christians to them, making them trust you and love you, by pleasing them, giving way to them, making yourself of service to them, doing what they like whenever you can, in order that they may do to you, as you have done to them, and measure back to you (as the Lord Jesus promises they will), with the same measure with which you have measured to them. In short, serving men, that you may rule them, and stooping before them that you may conquer them.

And if any of you are too proud to try this plan, and think it fairer to drive men than to lead them, I can tell you of two persons who were not as proud as you are, and were not ashamed to do what you are ashamed to do—and yet they are two persons, before the least of whom you would hang your head, and feel, as I am sure I should, a very small, and mean, and pitiful person if I met them in the road.

For the first, and by far the least of the two, is St. Paul. Now St. Paul says this was the very plan by which he got influence over men, and persuaded and converted them, and brought them home to God, by being himself a servant to all men, and pleasing all men, being a Jew to the Jews, and a Greek to the Greeks, and all things to all men, if by any means he might save some. Giving up, giving way, taking trouble, putting himself out of the way, as we say here, all day long, to win people to love him, and trust him, and see that he really cared for them, and therefore to be ready to listen to him. From what one can see of St. Paul's manners, from his own Epistles, he must have been the most perfect gentleman; a gentle man, civil, obliging, delicate minded, careful to hurt no one's feelings; and when he had (as he had often) to say rough things and deal with rough men, doing it as tenderly and carefully as he could, like his Master the Lord Jesus Christ, lest he should break the bruised reed, or quench the smoking flax. Which of us can read the Epistle to Philemon (which to my mind is the most civil, pleasant, kindly, gentlemanlike speech which I know on earth), without saying to ourselves, "Ah, if we had but St. Paul's manners, St. Paul's temper, St. Paul's way of managing people, how few quarrels there would be in this noisy troublesome world."

But I said that there was one greater than St. Paul who was not ashamed to behave in the very same way, stooping to all, conciliating all. And so there is—One whose shoes St. Paul was not worthy to stoop down and unloose—and that is, the Lord Jesus Christ Himself—who ate and drank with publicans and sinners, who went out into the highways and hedges, to bring home into God's kingdom poor wretches whom men despised and cast off. It was He who taught St. Paul to behave in the same way. May He teach us to behave in the same way also! St. Paul learnt to discern men's spirits, and feel for them, and understand them, and help them, and comfort them, and at last to turn and change them whichever way he chose, simply because he was full of the Spirit of Christ, who is the Spirit of God, proceeding both from the Father and the Son.

For St. Paul says positively, that his reason for not pleasing himself, but taking so much trouble to please other people, was because Christ also pleased not Himself. "We that are strong," he says, "ought to bear the infirmities of the weak, and not to please ourselves. Let every man please his neighbour for his good unto edification, for even Christ pleased not Himself," (Rom. xv. 1-3.) And again, "We have a High Priest who can be touched with the feeling of our infirmities," (Heb. iv. 15). So it was by stooping to men, that Christ learned to understand men, and by understanding men He was able to save men. And again, St. Paul says, "Let this mind be in you which was also in Christ Jesus, who being in the form of God, and equal with God," yet—"made Himself of no reputation, but took upon Him the form of a slave, and was made in the likeness of man, and being found in fashion as a man, humbled Himself, and became obedient unto death, even the death of the cross," (Phil. ii. 5, 9, 10).

There, my friends—there was the perfect fulfilment of the great law—Stoop to conquer. There was the reward of Christ's not pleasing Himself. Christ stooped lower than any man, and therefore He rose again higher than all men. He did more to please men than any man; and therefore God was better pleased with Him than with all men, and a voice came from Heaven, saying—This Person who stoops to the lowest depths that He may understand and help those who were in the lowest deep—this outcast who has not where to lay His head, slandered, blasphemed, spit on, scourged, crucified, because He will help all, and feel for all, and preach to all; "this is my beloved Son, in whom I am well pleased," (Matt. iii. 17). "The brightness of my glory,—the express image of my person,"(Heb. i.3).

My friends, this may seem to you a strange sermon, which began by talking of railroads and steamships, and ends by talking of the death and the glory of the Lord Jesus Christ; and you may ask what has the end of it to do with the beginning?

If you want to know, recollect that I began by saying that there was but One wisdom for earth or heaven, for man and for God; and that is the wisdom which lies in stooping to conquer, as the Lord Jesus Christ did. Think over that, and behave accordingly; and be sure, meanwhile, that whenever you feel proud, and self-willed, and dictatorial, and inclined to drive men instead of leading them, and to quarrel with them, instead of trying to understand them and love them, and bring them round gently, by appealing to their reason and good feeling, not to their fear of you—then you are going not God's way, no, nor man's way either, but the devil's way. You are going, not the way by which the Lord Jesus Christ rose to Heaven, but the way by which the devil fell from Heaven, as all self-willed proud men will fall. Proud and self-willed men will not get done the things they want to be done; while the meek, those who are gentle, and tender, and try to draw men as God does with the cords of a man and the bands of love, will prosper in this world and in the next; they will see their heart's desire; they will inherit the land, and be refreshed in the multitude of peace.

XIX

IT IS GOOD FOR THE YOUNG TO REJOICE

"Rejoice, O young man, in thy youth; and let thy heart cheer thee in the days of thy youth, and walk in the ways of thine heart, and in the sight of thine eyes: but know thou, that for all these things God will bring thee into judgment."—Ecclesiastes xi. 9.

Some people fancy that in this text God forbids young people to enjoy themselves. They think that the words are spoken ironically, and with a sneer, as if to say,

"Yes. Enjoy yourself if you will. Go your own way if you wish. Make a fool of yourself if you are determined to do so. You will repent it at last. You will be caught at last, and punished at last."

Now, I cannot think that there would be in Scripture or in any word of God a sneer so cruel and so unjust as that. For surely it would be unjust of God, if after giving young people the power to be happy, He then punished them for being happy, for using the very powers which He had given them, obeying the very feelings which He had implanted in them, enjoying the very pleasures which He had put in their way. God cannot be a tempter, my friends. He does not surely send us into a world full of traps and snares, and then punish us for being caught in the very snares which He had set. God forbid. Let us never fancy such things of God the heavenly Father, from whom comes every good and perfect gift. Let us leave such fancies for soured and hard-hearted persons, who make a god in their own likeness—a god of darkness and not of light—a grudger and not a giver. And let us take this text literally and plainly as it stands, and see whether we cannot learn from it a really wholesome lesson.

"Rejoice! oh, young man, in thy youth."

The Bible tells you to rejoice, therefore do so without fear. God has given you health, strength, spirits, hope, the power of enjoyment. And why, save but that you may enjoy them, and rejoice in your youth? He has given you more health, more strength, more spirits, than you need to earn your daily bread, or to learn your daily task. And why? To enable you to grow in body and in soul. And that you will only do if you are happy. The human soul, says a wise man, is like a plant, and requires sunshine to make it grow and ripen. And the heavenly Father has given you sunshine in your hearts that you may grow into hearty, healthy-minded men. If young people have not sunshine enough, if they are kept down and crushed in youth by sorrow, by anxiety, by fear, by over-hard work, by too much study, by strict and cruel masters, by dark and superstitious notions about God's anger, by over-scrupulousness about this and that thing being sinful, then their souls and minds do not grow; they become more or less stunted, unhealthy, unhappy, slavish, and mean people in after-life, because they have not rejoiced in their youth as God intended them to do.

Remember this, you parents, and be sure that all harshness and cruelty to your children, all terrifying of them, all over-working of them, body or mind, all making them unhappy by requiring of them more than the plain law of God requires; or by teaching them to dread, not to love, their Father in heaven—All these will stunt and hurt their characters in after-life; and all are, therefore, sins against their heavenly Father, who willeth not that one little one should perish, and who will require a strict account of each of us how we have brought up the children whom He has committed to our charge. Let their hearts cheer them in the days of their youth. They will have trouble enough, anxiety enough hereafter. Do not you forestall the evil days for them. The more cheerful their growth is the more heart and spirit they will have to face the trials and sorrows of life when they come.

But further, the text says to the young man, Walk in the ways of thy heart. That is God's permission to free men, in a free country. You are not slaves either to man or to God; and God does not treat you as slaves, but as children whom He can trust. He says, Walk in the ways of thine own heart. Do what you will, provided it be not wrong. Choose your own path in life. Exert yourselves boldly to better yourselves in any path you choose, which is not a path of dishonesty and sin.

Again, says the text, Walk in the sight of thine eyes. As your bodies are free, let your minds be free likewise. See for yourselves, judge for yourselves. God has given you eyes, brains, understanding; use them. Get knowledge for yourselves, get experience for yourselves. Educate and cultivate your own minds. Live, as far as you can, a free, reasonable, cheerful, happy life, enjoying this world, if you feel able to enjoy it. But know thou, that for all these things, God will bring thee into judgment.

Ah! say some, there is the sting. How can we enjoy ourselves if we are to be brought into judgment after all?

My friends, before I answer that question, let me ask one. Do you look on God as a taskmaster, requiring of you, as the Egyptians did of the Jews, to make bricks all day without straw, and noting down secretly every moment that you take your eyes off your work, that He may punish you for it years hence when you have forgotten it—extreme to mark what is done amiss?

Or do you look on God as a Father who rejoices in the happiness of His children?—Who sets them no work to do but what is good for them, and requires them to do nothing without giving them first the power and the means to do it?—A Father who knows our necessities before we ask for help and a Saviour who is able and willing to give us help? If you think of God in that former way as a stern taskmaster, I can tell you nothing about Him. I know Him not; I find Him neither in the Bible, in the world, nor in my own conscience and reason. He is not the God of the Bible, the God of the Gospel whom I am commanded to preach to you.

But if you think of God as a Father, as your Father in heaven, who chastens you in His love that you may partake of His holiness, and of His Son Jesus Christ as your Saviour, your Lord, who loves you, and desires your salvation, body and soul—of Him I can speak; for He is the True and only God, revealed by His Son Jesus Christ our Lord; and in His light I can tell you to rejoice and take comfort, ever though He brings you into judgment; for being your Father in heaven, He can mean nothing but your good, and He would not bring you into judgment if that too was not good for you.

Now, you must remember that the judgment of which Solomon speaks here is a judgment in this life. The whole Book of Ecclesiastes, from which the text is taken, is about this life. Solomon says so specially, and carefully. He is giving here advice to his son; and his doctrine all through is, that a man's happiness or misery in this life, his good or bad fortune in this life, depend almost entirely on his own conduct; and, above all, on his conduct in youth. As a man sows he shall reap, is his doctrine.

Therefore, he says, in this very chapter, Do what if right, just because it is right. It is sure to pay you in the long run, somehow, somewhere, somewhen. Cast thy bread on the waters—that is, do a generous thing whenever you have an opportunity—and thou shalt find it after many days. Give a portion to seven, and also to eight, for thou knowest not what evil shall be on the earth. Every action of yours will bear fruit. Every thing you do, and every word you say, will God bring into judgment, sooner or later. It will rise up against you, years afterwards, to punish you, or it will rise up for you, years afterwards, to reward you. It must be so, says Solomon; that is the necessary, eternal, moral law of God's world. As you do, so will you be rewarded. If the clouds be full of rain, they must empty themselves on the earth. Where the tree falls, there it will lie. As we say in England, as you make your bed, so you will lie on it. That does not (as people are too apt to think) speak of what is to happen to us after we die. It speaks expressly and only of what will happen before we die. It is the same as our English proverb.

Therefore, he says, do not look too far forward. Do not be double-minded, doing things with a mean and interested after-thought, plotting, planning, asking, will this right thing pay me or not? He that observeth the wind, and is too curious and anxious about the weather, will not sow; and he that regardeth the clouds shall not reap. No; just do the right thing which lies nearest you, and trust to God to prosper it. In the morning sow thy seed, and in the evening withhold not thine hand; for thou knowest not which shall prosper, this or that, or whether they shall both be alike good. Thou knowest not, he says, the works of God, who maketh all. All thou knowest is, that the one only chance of success in life is to fear God and keep His commandments, for this is the whole duty of man. For God shall bring every work into judgment, with every secret thing, whether it be good, or whether it be evil.

Whether it be good, or whether it be evil.

He does not say only that God will bring your evil deeds into judgment. But that He will bring your good ones also, and your happiness and good fortune in this life will be, on the whole, made up of the sum-total of the good and harm you have done, of the wisdom or the folly which you have thought and carried out. It is so. You know it is so. When you look round on other men, you see that on the whole men prosper very much as they deserve. There are exceptions, I know. Solomon knew that well. Such strange and frightful exceptions, that one must believe that those who have been so much wronged in this life will be righted in the life to come. Children suffer for the sins of their parents. Innocent people suffer with the guilty. But these are the exceptions, not the rule. And these exceptions are much more rare than we choose to confess. When a man complains to you that he has been unfortunate, that the world has been unjust to him, that he has not had fair play in life, and so forth, in three cases out of four you will find that it is more or less the man's own fault; that he has deserved his losses, that is, earned them for himself. I do not mean that the man need have been a wicked man—not in the least. But he has been imprudent, perhaps weak, hasty, stupid, or something else; and his faults, perhaps some one fault, has hampered him, thrown him back, and God has brought him to judgment for it, and made it punish him. And why? Surely that he may see his fault and repent of it, and mend it for the time to come.

I say, God may bring a man's fault into judgment, and let it punish him, without the man being a bad man. And you, young people, will find in after-life that you will have earned, deserved, merited, and worked out for yourselves a great deal of your own happiness and misery.

I know this seems a hard doctrine. People are always ready to lay their misfortunes on God, on the world, on any and every one, rather than on themselves.

A bad education, for instance—a weakly constitution which some bring into the world, with or without any fault of their own, are terrible drawbacks and sore afflictions. The death of those near and dear to us, of which we cannot always say, I have earned this, I have brought it on myself. It is the Lord. Let Him do what seemeth Him good.

But because misfortunes may come upon us without our own fault, that is no reason why we should not provide against the misfortunes which will be our own fault. Nay, is it not all the stronger reason for providing against them, that there are other sorrows against which we cannot provide? Alas! is there not misery horrible enough hanging over our heads daily in this mortal life without our making more for ourselves by our own folly? We shall have grief enough before we die without adding to that grief the far bitterer torment of remorse!

Oh, young people, young people, listen to what I say! You can be, you will be, you must be, the builders of your own good or bad fortunes. On you it depends whether your lives shall be honourable and happy, or dishonourable and sad. There is no such thing as luck or fortune in this world. What is called Fortune is nothing else than the orderly and loving providence of the Lord Jesus Christ, who orders all things in heaven and earth, and who will, sooner or later, reward every man according to his works. Just in proportion as you do the will of your Father in heaven, just so far will doing His will bring its own blessing and its own reward.

Instead of hoping for good fortune which may never come, or fearing bad fortune which may never come either, pray, each of you, for the Holy Spirit of God, the Spirit of right-doing, which is good fortune in itself; good fortune in this world; and in the world to come, everlasting life. Fear God and keep His commandments, and all will be well. For who is the man who is master of his own luck? The Psalmist tells us, in Psalm xv., "He that leadeth an uncorrupt life, and doeth the thing which is right, and speaketh the truth from his heart." "He that backbiteth not with his tongue, nor doeth evil to his neighbour, nor taketh up a reproach against his neighbour. In whose eyes a vile person is contemned; but he honoureth them that fear the Lord: he that sweareth to his own hurt, and changeth not. He that putteth not out his money to usury, nor taketh reward against the innocent."

Whoso doeth these things shall never fall. And as long as you are doing those things, you may rejoice freely and heartily in your youth, believing that the smile of God, who gave you the power of being happy, is on your happiness; and that your heavenly Father no more grudges harmless pleasure to you, than He grudges it to the gnat which dances in the sunbeam, or the bird which sings upon the bough. For He is The Father,—and what greater delight to a father than to see his children happy, if only, while they are happy, they are good?

XX

GOD'S BEAUTIFUL WORLD.

A SPRING SERMON

"Bless the Lord, O my soul. O Lord my God, thou art very great: thou art clothed with honour and majesty. Who coverest thyself with light as with a garment: who stretchest out the heavens like a curtain: who layeth the beams of his chambers in the waters: who maketh the clouds his chariot: who walketh upon the wings of the wind."—Ps. civ. 1-3.

At this delicious season of the year, when spring time is fast ripening into summer, and every hedge, and field, and garden is full of life and growth, full of beauty and fruitfulness; and we look back on the long winter, and the boughs which stood bare so drearily for six months, as if in a dream; the blessed spring with its green leaves, and gay flowers, and bright suns has put the winter's frosts out of our thoughts, and we seem to take instinctively to the warmth, as if it were our natural element—as if we were intended, like the bees and butterflies, to live and work only in the summer days, and not to pass, as we do in this climate, one-third of the year, one-third of our whole lives, in mist, cold, and gloom. Now, there is a meaning in all this—in our love of bright, warm weather, a very deep and blessed meaning in it. It is a sign to us where we come from—where God would have us go. A sign that we came from God's heaven of light and beauty, that God's heaven of light and beauty is meant for us hereafter. That love which we have for spring, is a sign, that we are children of the everlasting Spring, children of the light and of the day, in body and in soul; if we would but claim our birthright!

For you must remember that mankind came from a warm country—a country all of sunshine and joy. Adam in the garden of Eden was in no cold or severe climate, he had no need of clothes, not even of the trouble of tilling the ground. The bountiful earth gave him all he wanted. The trees over his head stretched out the luscious fruits to him—the shady glades were his only house, the mossy banks his only bed. He was bred up the child of sunshine and joy. But he was not meant to stay there. God who brings good out of evil, gave man a real blessing when He drove him out of the garden of Eden. Men were meant to fill the earth and to conquer it, as they are doing at this day. They were meant to become hardy and industrious—to be forced to use their hands and their heads to the utmost stretch, to call out into practice all the powers which lay ready in them. They were meant, in short, according to the great law of God's world, to be made perfect through sufferings, and therefore it was God's kindness, and not cruelty, to our forefathers, when He sent them out into the world; and that He did not send them into any exceedingly hot country, where they would have become utterly lazy and profligate, like the negroes and the South Sea islanders, who have no need to work, because the perpetual summer gives them their bread ready-made to their hands. And it was a kindness, too, that God did not send our forefathers out into any exceedingly cold country, like the Greenlanders and the Esquimaux, where the perpetual winter would have made them greedy, and stunted, and stupid; but that He sent us into this temperate climate, where there is a continual change and variety of seasons. Here first, stern and wholesome winter, then bright, cheerful summer, each bringing a message and a lesson from our loving Father in heaven. First comes winter, to make us hardy and daring, and industrious, and strips the trees, and bares the fields, and takes away all food from the earth, and cries to us with the voice of its storms, "He that will not work, neither shall he eat." "Go to the ant, thou sluggard; consider her ways, and be wise: who layeth up her meat in the summer, and provideth her food against the time of frosts." And then comes summer, with her flowers and her fruits, and brings us her message from God, and says to us poor, slaving, hard-worn children of men, "You are not meant to freeze, and toil, and ache for ever. God loves to see you happy; God is willing to feed your eyes with fair sights, your bodies with pleasant food, to cheer your hearts with warmth and sunshine as much as is good for you. He does not grieve willingly, nor afflict the children of men. See the very bees and gnats, how they dance and bask in the sunbeams! See the very sparrows, how they choose their mates and build their nests, and enjoy themselves as if they were children of the spring! And are not ye of more value than many sparrows? you who can understand and enjoy the spring, you men and women who can understand and enjoy God's fair earth ten thousand times more than those dumb creatures can. It is for you God has made the spring. It is for your sakes that Christ, the ruler of the earth, sends light and fruitfulness, and beauty over the world year by year. And why? Not merely to warm and feed your bodies, but to stir up your hearts with grateful love to Him, the Blessed One, and to teach you what you are to expect from Him hereafter."

Ay, my friends, this is the message the spring and summer bring with them—they are signs and sacraments from God, earnests of the everlasting spring—the world of unfading beauty and perpetual happiness which is the proper home of man, which God has prepared for those that love Him—the world wherein there shall be no more curse, neither sorrow nor sighing, but the Lord God and the Lamb shall be the light thereof; and the rivers of that world shall be waters of life, and the trees of that world shall be for the healing of the nations; and the children of the Lord God shall see Him face to face, and be kings and priests to Him for ever and ever. Therefore, I say, rejoice in spring time, and in the sights, and sounds, and scents which spring time, as a rule, brings; and remember, once for all, never lose an opportunity of seeing anything beautiful. Beauty is God's hand-writing—God's image. It is a wayside sacrament, a cup of blessing; welcome it in every fair landscape, every fair face, every fair flower, and drink it in with all your eyes, and thank Christ for it, who is Himself the well-spring of all beauty, who giveth all things richly to enjoy.

I think, this 104th Psalm is a fit and proper psalm to preach on in this sweet spring time; for it speaks, from beginning to end, of God's earth, and of His glory, and love, and wisdom which shines forth on this earth. And though, at first sight, it may not seem to have much to do with Christianity, and with the great mystery of our redemption, yet, I believe and know that it has at bottom all and everything to do with it; that this 104th Psalm is as full of comfort and instruction for Christian men as any other Psalm in the whole Bible. I believe that without feeling rightly and healthily about this Psalm, we shall not feel rightly or healthily about any other part of the Bible, either Old or New Testament. At all events God's inspired psalmist was not ashamed to write this psalm. God's Spirit thought it worth while to teach him to write this psalm. God's providence thought it worth while to preserve this psalm for us in His holy Bible, and therefore I think it must be worth while for us to understand this psalm, unless we pretend to be wiser than God. I have no fancy for picking and choosing out of the holy Bible; all Scripture is given by inspiration of God—all Scripture is profitable for doctrine, for reproof, for correction, for instruction in righteousness, and therefore this 104th Psalm is profitable as well as the rest; and especially profitable to be explained in a few sermons as I said before, at this season when, if we have any eyes to see with, or hearts to feel with, we ought to be wondering at and admiring God's glorious earth, and saying, with the old prophet in my text, "Praise the Lord, O my soul. O Lord my God, thou art very great; thou art clothed with honour and majesty. Who coverest thyself with light as with a garment: who stretchest out the heavens as with a curtain: who layeth the beams of his chambers in the waters: who maketh the clouds his chariot: who walketh upon the wings of the wind . . . O Lord, how manifold are thy works! in wisdom hast thou made them all: the earth is full of thy riches" (Ps. civ. 1, 2, 3, 24).

First, then, consider those wonderful words of the text, how God covers Himself with light as it were with a garment. Truly there is something most divine in light; it seems an especial pattern and likeness of God. The Bible uses it so continually. Light is a pattern of God's wisdom; for light sees into everything, searches through everything, and light is a pattern of God's revelation, for light shows us everything; without light our eyes would be useless—and so without God our soul's eyes would be useless. It is God who teaches us all we know. It is God who makes us understand all we understand. He opens the meaning of everything to us, just as the light shews everything to us; and as in the sunlight only we see the brightness and beauty of the earth, so it is written, "In thy light, O God, we shall see light." Thus light is God's garment. It shows Him to us, and yet it hides Him from us. Who could dare or bear to look on God if we saw Him as He is face to face? Our souls would be dazzled blind, as our eyes are by the sun at noonday. But now, light is a pattern to us of God's glory; and therefore it is written, that light is God's garment, that God dwells in the light which no man can approach unto. As a wise old heathen nobly said, "Light is the shadow of God;" and so, as the text says, He stretches out those glorious blue heavens above us as a curtain and shield, to hide our eyes from His unutterable splendour, and yet to lift our souls up to Him. The vastness and the beauty of those heavens, with all their countless stars, each one a sun or a world in itself, should teach us how small we are, how great is our Father who made all these.

When we see a curtain, and know that it bides something beautiful behind it, our curiosity and wonder is awakened, and we long all the more to see what is behind that curtain. So the glory of those skies ought to make us wonder and long all the more to see the God who made the skies.

But again, the Psalmist says that God lays the beams of His chambers in the waters, and makes the clouds His chariot, and walks upon the wings of the wind! that He makes His angels the storms, and His ministers a flaming fire. You must not suppose that the psalmist had such a poor notion of the great infinite God, as to fancy that He could be in any one place. God wants no chambers—even though they were built of the clouds, arched with rainbows, as wide as the whole vault of heaven. He wants no wind to carry Him—He carries all things and moves all things. In Him they live, and move, and have their being. Yet Him—the heaven, and the heaven of heavens cannot contain Him! He is everywhere and no where—for He is a Spirit; He is in all things, and yet He is no thing—for He was before all things, and in Him all things consist. He is the Absolute, the Uncreated, the Infinite, the One and the All. And the old Psalmist knew that as well as we do, perhaps better. What, then, did he mean by these two last verses? He meant, that in all those things God was present—that the world was not like a machine, a watch, which God had wound up at the creation, and started off to go of itself; but that His Spirit, His providence, were guiding everything, even as at the first. That those mists and rain came from Him, and went where He sent them; that those clouds carried His blessings to mankind; that when the thunder shower bursts on one parish, and leaves the next one dry, it is because God will have it so; that He brings the blessed purifying winds out of His treasures, to sweeten and fatten the earth with the fresh breath of life, which they have drunk up from the great Atlantic seas, and from the rich forests of America—that they blow whither He thinks best; that clouds and rain, wind and lightning, are His fruitful messengers and His wholesome ministers, fulfilling His word, each according to their own laws, but also each according to His especial providence, who has given the whole earth to the children of men. This is the meaning of the Psalmist, that the weather is not a dead machine, but a living, wonderful work of the Spirit of God, the Lord and giver of life. Therefore we may dare to pray for fair and seasonable weather; we may dare to pray against blight and tempest—humbly, because we know not what is altogether good for us,—but boldly and freely, because we know that there is a living, loving God, governing the weather, who does know what is good for us; who has given us His only begotten Son, and will with Him also give us all things.

And so ends my first sermon on the 104th Psalm.

XXI

WONDERS OF THE SEA

OR

DAILY MIRACLES

"Thou coverest the earth with the deep sea as with a garment."—Psalm civ. 6.

When we look at a map of the world, one of the first things that strikes us as curious is, how little dry land there is, and how much sea. More than half the world covered with deep, wild, raging, waste salt water! It seems very strange. Of what use to man can all that sea be? And yet the Scripture says that the whole earth has God given to the children of men. And therefore He has given to us the sea which is part of the earth. But of what use is the sea to us?

We are ready to say at first sight, "How much better if the world had been all dry land? There would have been so much more space for men to spread on—so much more land to grow corn on. What is the use of all that sea?" But when we look into the matter, we shall find, that every word of God stands true, in every jot and tittle of it—that we ought to thank God for the sea as much as for the land—that David spoke truly when he said, in this Psalm civ., that the great and wide sea also is full of God's riches.

For in the first place—What should we do without water? Not only to drink, but to feed all trees, and crops which grow. Those who live in a dry parish know well the need of water for the crops. In fact, strange as it may seem, out of water is made wood. You know, perhaps, that plants are made out of the salts in the soil—but not only out of salts—they are made also out of water. Every leaf and flower is made up only of those two things—salts from the soil, and water from the sky. Most wonderful! But so it is. Water is made up of several very different things. The leaves and flowers, when they drink up water, keep certain parts of water, and turn them into wood; and the part of the water which they do not want, is just the part which we do want, namely, fresh air, for water is full of fresh air. And therefore the plants breathe out the fresh air through their leaves, that we may breathe it into our lungs. More and more wonders, you see, as we go on!

But where does all the rain water and spring water come from? From the clouds. And where do the clouds come from? From the Sea. The sea water is drawn up by the sun's heat, evaporated, as we call it, into the air, and makes mist, and that mist grows together into clouds. And these clouds empty their blessed life-giving treasures on the land—to feed man, and beast, and herb.

But what is it which governs these clouds, and makes them do their appointed work? The Psalmist tells us, "At Thy rebuke they flee; at the voice of Thy thunder they are afraid." He gives the same account of it which wise men now-a-days give. It is God, he says, and the Providence of God, which raises the clouds, and makes them water the earth. And the means which He employs is thunder. Now this is strictly true. We all know that thunder gathers the clouds together, and brings rain: but we do not all know that the power which makes the thunder, which we call electricity, is working all around us everywhere. It is only when it bursts out, in flame and noise, which we call lightning and thunder, that we perceive it—but it is still there, this wonderful thing called electricity, for ever at work—giving the clouds their shape, making them fly with vast weights of water through the sky, and then making them pour down that water in rain.

But there is another deep meaning in those words of the Psalmist's about thunder. He tells us that at the voice of God's thunder the waters are afraid—that He has set them their bounds which they shall not pass, nor turn again to cover the earth. And it is true. Also that it is this same thunder power which makes dry land—for there is thunder beneath us, and lightning too, in the bowels of the earth. Those who live near burning mountains know this well. They see not only flames, but real lightning, real thunder playing about the burning mouths of the fiery mountains—they hear the roaring, the thundering of the fire-kingdom miles beneath their feet, under the solid crust of the earth. And they see, too, whole hills, ay, whole counties, sometimes, heaved up many feet in a single night, by this thunder under ground—and islands thrown up in the midst of the sea—so that where there was once deep water is now dry land.

Now, in this very way, strange as it may seem, almost all dry land is made. This whole country of England once lay at the bottom of the sea. You may now see shells and sea fishes bedded in high rocks and hill tops. But it was all heaved up by the thunder which works under ground. There are places in England where I have seen the marks of the fire on the rocks; and the solid stone crushed, and twisted, and melted by the vast force of the fire which thrust up the land from beneath—and thus the land was heaved up from under the waters, and the sea fled away and left its old bed dry—firm land and high cliffs—and as the Psalmist says, "At the voice of God's thunder the waters were afraid. Thou hast set them their bounds which they shall not pass, neither turn again to cover the earth."

Wonderful as all this may seem, all learned men know that it is true. And this one thing at least it ought to teach us, what a wonderful and Almighty God we have to deal with, whose hand made all these things—and what a loving and merciful God, who makes not only the wind and the sea, and the thunder and the fire kingdoms obey Him, but makes their violence bring blessings to mankind. The fire kingdom heaves up dry land for men to dwell on—the thunder brings mellow rains—the winds sweep the air clean, and freshen all our breath—and feed the plants with rich air drawn from far forests in America, and from the wild raging seas—the sea sends up its continual treasures of rain—everywhere are harmony and fitness, beauty and use in all God's works. He has made nothing in vain. All His works praise Him, and surely, also, His saints should give thanks to Him! Oh! my friends—every thunder shower—every fresh south-west breeze, is a miracle of God's mercy, if we could but see thoroughly into it.

Consider, again, another wonderful proof of God's goodness in what we call the Tides of the sea. God has made the waters so, that they can never stand still—the sea is always moving. Twice a day it rises, and twice a day it sinks and ebbs again all along the shore. It would take too long to explain why this is—but it is enough to say, that it must be so, from the way in which God has made the earth and the water. So that it did not come from accident. God planned and intended it all when He made the sea at first. His all-foreseeing love settled it all. Now of what use are these tides? They keep the sea from rotting, by keeping it in a perpetual stir. And the sea, as it ebbs and flows, draws the air after it, and so keeps the air continually moving and blowing, therefore continually fresh, and continually carrying in it rich food for plants from one country to another. There are other reasons why the winds blow, which I have not time to mention now; but they all go to prove the same thing.—How wisely and well the Psalmist said, "Praise the Lord upon earth ye rivers and all deeps. Fire and hail, snow and vapour, wind and storm, fulfilling His word" (Ps. cxlviii.).

Another use of the sea, again, is the vast quantity of food which it gives. Labouring men who live inland have no notion of the wonderful fruitfulness of those seemingly barren wastes of water, or how many millions of human beings live mostly on fish. When we consider those great banks of Newfoundland, where fish enough perhaps to feed all England are caught every season, and sent over the whole world; our own herring fisheries, where thousands of millions of fish are caught yearly—and all the treasures of food and the creeping things innumerable, both small and great beasts, of which the Psalmist speaks; when we consider all this, we shall begin to bless God for the sea, as much as for the land.

"There go the ships," too, says the Psalmist, in this 104th Psalm, "and there goeth that leviathan, whom Thou hast made to take his pastime therein." This leviathan is no doubt the whale—the largest of all living things—often a hundred feet long, and as thick as a house. And yet even of him, the monster of all monsters, does God's Word stand true, that He has put all things under man's feet, that all things are in subjection to man—the fish of the sea, and whatsoever walketh through the paths of the sea. For even the great whale cannot stand before the cunning of man—God has taught man the means of killing even it, and turning it to his own use. The whalebone which we use, the oil which we burn in lamps, comes from the bodies of those enormous creatures which wander in the far seas like floating houses, ten thousand miles away.

But again, it is promised in the Bible, that in the new heavens and new earth there shall be no more sea. When the sea has done its work, God will have done with it—and then there will be no more division between nation and nation—no more long dangerous voyages from one country to another.

And strange to say—the sea is even now at work bringing about this very thing—destroying itself—filling itself up. Day by day the sea eats away its own shore, and banks, and carries down their remains to make its own bed shallower and shallower, till shoals and new lands arise where there was deep sea before. So that if the world lasts long enough, the sea by its own laws will be filled up, and dry land appear everywhere.

The bottom of the sea is full, too, of countless millions of strange insects—and yet even in these strange insects there is use; for not only do they give food to countless millions of fishes, but after a time they turn into stone, and form fruitful soil. There are now in many parts of the world great beds of rock and earth, many feet thick, and miles long, made up entirely out of the skeletons and shells of little insects which lived at the bottom of the sea thousands of years ago.

Are not these things wonderful? Well, then, remember who made these wonders? who keeps them working? Your Father—and the Son of God, and the Spirit of God. The Son of God—ay, think of Him—He by whom all things were made—He by whom all things consist—He to whom all power is given in heaven and earth. He came down and died on the cross for you. He calls to you to come and serve Him loyally and gratefully—dare you refuse Him—The Maker and King of this glorious world? He died for you. He loves you. He condescends to beseech you to come to Him that you may have life. Alas! what can you expect if you will not come to Him? How will you escape if you turn your back on your Maker, and despise your own Creator when He stoops to entreat you? Oh folly—Oh madness—Oh utter shame and ruin!

There are some people who do not like science and philosophy, because they say, If you try to explain to people, and make them understand the wonderful things around them, they will stop thinking them wonderful, and so you will spoil their reverence, and "familiarity will breed contempt." Now, no doubt a little learning is a dangerous thing, when it makes some shallow conceited fellow fancy he knows all about everything. But I can truly say, that the more you really do know about this earth, the more your astonishment at it will grow—for the more you understand about trees and animals, clouds and seas, the less you will find you understand about them. The more you read about them and watch them, the more infinitely and inexpressibly wonderful you find them, and the more you get humbled and awestruck at the boundless wisdom and love of Our Father in Heaven, and Christ the Word of God who planned and made this wondrous world, and the Holy Spirit of God who is working this wondrous world. I tell you, my friends, that as St. Paul says, "If a man will be wise, let him become a fool that he may be wise." Let him go about feeling how short-sighted, and stupid, and ignorant he is—and how infinitely wise Christ the Word of God is, by whom all things were made, to whom all belong. Let him go about wondering day and night, always astonished more and more, as everything he sees gives him some fresh proof of the glory of God; till he falls down on his knees and cries out with the Psalmist, "Lord, what is man that Thou art mindful of him, or the son of man, that Thou so regardest him?" When I consider Thy Heavens, even the work of Thine hands, I say, What is man? and yet Thou madest man to have dominion over the works of Thine hands, and hast put all things in subjection under his feet—the fowl of the air and the fishes of the sea, and whatsoever walketh through the paths of the seas. O Lord, our Governor, how excellent is Thy name in all the world. In comparison of Thee what is man's wisdom? What is man's power? Thou alone art glorious, for by Thee are all things, and for Thee they were made, and are created, that Thou mightest rejoice in the works of Thy own hands, and bless the creatures which Thy love has made!

XXII

THE SAILOR'S GOD.

PREACHED TO SAILORS AT A LITTLE FISHING VILLAGE IN CORNWALL, 1843

"They that go down to the sea in ships, and occupy their business in great waters; these men see the works of the Lord, and his wonders in the deep."—Ps. cvii. 23, 24.

My brothers—for though I do not know most of you even by name, yet you are still my brothers, for His sake in whose name you were baptized—my brothers, it has been often said that seamen and fishermen ought to be the most religious men in the country. And why? Because they, more than any set of men, see the works of the Lord, and His wonders in the deep.

The cotton-spinner, who is shut up in a factory all day long, with nothing before his eyes but his loom, and nothing to look at beyond his own house but dingy streets and smoking furnace chimneys—he, poor man, sees very little of the works of the Lord. Man made the world of streets and shops and machinery in which that poor workman lives and dies. What wonder is it if he forgets the God who made him—the God who made the round world, and set it so fast that it should not be moved, and has given the sea its bounds that it should not overflow them at any time? How much better off are you seamen than such a man as that!

And you are better off too, even, than most field labourers and farmers. They are not shut up in towns, it is true; they have God's beautiful earth to till and keep: but they are too safe on shore! Yes; it may seem a strange thing to say; but you ought to thank God that your trade is a dangerous one—you have more to put you in mind of God than the labouring man!

And why? In the first place, as I said, fishermen and sailors see more of the wonderful works of God than any other set of men. Man may cut and change the earth—mining and quarrying and building—till it hardly looks like God's earth, but he cannot change the sea! There it is, just as God made it at first. Millions of rivers have run into it, yet it is not over full; cliffs have been wearing away and falling into it for six thousand years, yet is it not filled up. Millions of vessels have been sailing over it, yet they have left no mark upon it; it seems unchangeable, like God who made it. What is the use of my praising the sea to you? Do you not all know it, and fear it, and love it too? and does it not put you in mind of God who made it? who made that mighty water for the use of men, and filled it with thousands of different kinds of fishes, and weeds, and wonderful things for your use and comfort; and who has made it so strong that it shall keep you always in awe and fear and watchfulness, looking to God to save you—and yet so gentle and calm that you can sail upon its bosom, and there find food for your families. Which of you, who has any godly heart in him, can help feeling, sometimes at least when at sea, that he is seeing the wonderful works of God!

I said that you ought to thank God that your trade was a dangerous one, and I said that the sea should always keep you in fear and watchfulness, and looking to God to preserve you. Now, do you not see how these two sayings go together, and make each other plain. You seamen and fishermen are in continual danger; your lives are in your hands every moment—the belaying of a sheet, the strength of a bit of canvas, the toughness of a deal board, may settle your fate in a moment, and make all the difference between life and death. If they are sound, you may go back to a happy home, and see wife and children coming to meet you when you run on shore at morning from your honest labour; and if they fail—if that weak cordage, and these planks, and thinner canvas, on which your lives depend, do but give way, what is left for you the next moment? what but a grave in the deep, deep sea, and your wives widows and your children orphans, and your bodies devoured by ugly creeping things, and your souls gone—gone where? My good men—you who sit around me now so strong and full of life and skill and happiness—where would your souls be if you were drowned at sea to-morrow?

What a question! Oh, ask it yourselves honestly! I have been out in gales myself, and I cannot understand how you can go out, in thirty feet of timber, upon that mighty sea, with the wind howling over your heads like a death-bell, and the great hungry waves chasing you for miles, each one able and willing to swallow you up into the deep, and the gulls screaming over you as if they were waiting to feed upon your floating carcases, and you alone, in a tiny boat, upon that waste, howling wilderness of waters!—I cannot understand, I say, how, when a man is in such a case as that, day after day, year after year, he can forget his God, the only friend who can save him from the sea! the only friend who can send him safe out to his work in the evening, and bring him home safe to his wife at morning. One would think that when you went down to the shore in the morning, you would say, "Oh, God! without whose help I am no stronger than a piece of sea-weed floating up and down, take care of me! Take care of my wife and my children; and forgive me my sins, and do not punish me by calling me away this night to answer for them all!" And when you come home at night, you would say, "Oh, God! who hast kept me safe all this day, what can I do to show how thankful I am to Thee!" Ay! what can you do to show how thankful you are to God for His care? What ought you to do to show your thankfulness to Him? What must you do to show your thankfulness to Him? He has told you. "If you love me, He says, keep my commandments. Do justly, love mercy, and walk humbly with thy God."

These, my friends, are the holy and thankful thoughts which ought to be in your hearts every day and hour. This is the thought which God meant to put into your hearts when He made sailors of you, and brought you into the world, by the sea-side, to take up your business in great waters. You might have been born in Bristol or Liverpool or London, and never seen anything but streets and houses, and man's clumsy work. But God has been very good to you. He has brought you up here, in this happy West country, where you may see His wonderful works day and night; where you ought never to forget that you have a Father in heaven who made the sea, and who keeps you safe at sea by night and day. God has given you a great deal. He has given you two books to read—the book of God's Word, the Bible, and the book of God's earth, the sky and sea and land, which is above you and below you and around you day and night. If you can read and understand them properly, you will find in them everything which you want; you may learn from them to be holy in this world and happy in the next. God has given you, too, fathers, mothers, wives, children, a comfortable home, a holy trade—the same which the apostles followed. God has given you England for your country, and the West country—the best place in England for your home. God has given you a good Queen, and good magistrates and landlords. God has given you health and strength, and seamanship, and clear heads and stout hearts. And God has made you seamen and fishermen, and given you a business in which you can see God's mighty power and wisdom day and night, and feel Him taking care of you when you cannot take care of yourselves.

Therefore you ought to thank God that yours is a dangerous business, because it teaches you to trust in God alone for safety. And what are you to give Him in return? What does God require of you? You cannot pay Him back again for all His mercies, for they are past counting, but you must pay Him back all you can. And what must you pay Him back? First, you must trust in God; for he who comes to God and wishes to walk with God through life, as a good man should, must believe that there is a God, and that He will reward those who look to Him.

I never heard of a sailor who did not believe in God; for how can a man look at the sea, and not say to himself, God made the sea! But I have seen a great many sailors who did not trust in God. As long as it is fine weather, and everything goes right, they will forget God, and fancy that it is their own seamanship, and not God alone, which keeps their boats afloat, and their own skill in fishing, and not God alone, which sends the shoals of fish into their nets; and so they are truly fine-weather sailors—men who are only fit for calm seas and light breezes, when they can take care of themselves without God's help; but when a squall comes their hearts change, by God's mercy. For when a man has done all he can to save himself, and all he can do is no use, and his nets are adrift, and his boat on her beam ends, and the foaming rocks are on his lee, then he comes to his senses at last, and prays. Why did he not pray before? Why did he not save himself from all that misery and trouble and danger by thanking God for taking care of him, and praying to God to take care of him still. "Foolish men are plagued for their offences, and because of their wickedness. They that go down to the sea in ships, and occupy their business on great waters; these men see the works of the Lord, and His wonders in the deep; for at His word the stormy wind ariseth which lifteth up the waves thereof; they are carried up to heaven, and down again into the deep; their soul melteth away because of the trouble; they reel to and fro, and stagger like a drunken man, and are at their wit's end." And justly they are punished for forgetting God. God made the calm as well as the storm. Could they not remember that? But look at God's mercy; for when they cry unto the Lord in their trouble, He delivers them out of all their distress. For He makes the storm to cease, so that the waves are still; then are they glad because they are at rest, and so God brings them to the harbour where they would be.

Is there an old man sitting here who has not had this happen to him? And what did you do, my friend, when God had saved you out of that danger? It is easy to tell what you ought to have done; you ought to have gone home and fallen on your knees, and prayed to God; you ought to have said, Oh, Lord, I am a miserable, foolish sinner, who can only remember Thee when Thou art angry; an ungrateful son, who only thinks of his father when he beats him!

Oh, God, forgive me, I ought to have trusted in Thee before! I deserved all my danger and punishment and more. I did not deserve to be pardoned and saved from it! I deserve to be at the bottom of the sea at this moment. But forgive me, forgive me, loving and merciful Father, for the sake of Thy dear Son Jesus Christ, who died on the cross that I might be saved from death!

And when you had prayed thus, the next thing you ought to have asked yourself was—What does God require of me? how can I try to pay Him back—how can I show that I am thankful? My good friends, what does God require of you? "To do justly, and to love mercy, and to walk humbly with your God." I told you He required of you first to trust in Him at all hours, in all weathers. This is the next thing which He requires of you—To do justly, to cheat no man, not in the price of a pilchard; to love mercy; to love your neighbours, as Christ loved you; to help your neighbours, as Christ helped you and all mankind, by dying to save you; and as Christ has helped you, night after night, when you might have been buried in the waves, if Christ had not prayed for you that you might have time to repent, and bring forth fruits fit for repentance. To love mercy; to forgive every man who hurts you, for they are all Christian men and your brothers. Christ loved every one! Why should not you? If your wife or friend loved anything, you would be kind to it for their sakes; and so, if you really love God, and are thankful to Him for all His mercy and kindness, you will love every man you meet, for God's sake, who loved them and gave His Son for them.

"To walk humbly with your God." That is the beginning and end of all—you must be humble; you must confess that you are foolish, and God alone is wise; that you are weak, and God alone is strong; that you are poor fishermen, whom any squall may drown, and that God is the Great, Loving, Almighty God, who made heaven and earth, and the sea and all that is therein, and who helps all those who put their trust in Him. This is what God asks you to do in return for all He has done for you! To pray to Him, to praise Him, to put your trust in Him, to keep His commandments like thankful, humble, obedient, loving children. They who do these things, and only they, shall never fail. By night and day, in summer and winter, in storm and calm, in health and sickness, in richness and poverty, God will be with them. Christ will be with them. He sat in a fisherman's boat once, on the sea of Tiberias, and He will sit in your boats if you will but ask Him. He will steer you, He will save you, He will take care of your wives and children when you are far away, and He will bring you through the troublesome waves of this mortal life, so that, having faith for your anchor, and hope for your sail, and charity for your crew, you may at last land on the happy shore of everlasting life, there to live with God, world without end. God grant it may be so!

My good brothers—for I am a Christian like you, and an Englishman like you, and a west countryman like you—I thank our Father in heaven that He has brought me from the other end of England, and put this message into my mouth, to remind you of who you are—that you are the men who see the works of the Lord, and His wonders in the deep; and that God will say to every one of you at the day of judgment,—I taught you all this, I gave you all this, I did all this for you, what have you done for Me in return?

Go home—read over these verses in 107th Psalm, and think over what I have said. Do it to-night, for the weather has broken up—there are gales coming. Which of you can say that he will be alive next Sunday?

XXIII

THE GOOD SOLDIER OF JESUS CHRIST

"Thou therefore endure hardship as a good soldier of Jesus Christ."—2 Timothy ii. 3.

Suppose a young man went of his own will for a soldier; was regularly sworn in to serve the Queen; took his bounty; wore the Queen's uniform; ate her bread; learnt his drill; and all that a soldier need learn, as long as peace lasted. But suppose that, as soon as war came, and his regiment was ordered on active service, he deserted at once, and went off and hid himself. What should you call such a man? You would call him a base and ungrateful coward, and you would have no pity on him, if he was taken and justly punished.

But suppose that he did a worse thing still. Suppose that the enemy, the Russians say, invaded England, and the army was called out to fight them; and suppose this man of whom I speak, be he soldier or sailor, instead of fighting the enemy, deserted over to them, and fought on their side against his own country, and his own comrades, and his own father and brothers, what would you call that man? No name would be bad enough for him. If he was taken, he would be hanged without mercy, as not only a deserter but a traitor. And who would pity him or say that he had not got his just deserts?

Now, for God's sake and your own sakes consider. Are not all young people, when they are old enough to choose between right and wrong, if they choose what is wrong and live bad lives instead of good ones, very like this same deserter and traitor?

For are you not all Christ's soldiers, every one of you? Did not Christ enlist every one of you into His army, that, as the baptism service says, you might fight manfully under His banner against sin, the world, and the devil,—in one word, against all that is wrong and bad? And now when you are old enough to know that you are Christ's soldiers, what will you deserve to be called, if instead of fighting on Christ's side against what is good, you forget you are in His service? What are you but deserters from Christ's banner and army, traitors to Christ's cause?

But some may say, "My case is not like that soldier's. I did not enter Christ's service of my own free will. My parents put me into it when I was an infant, without asking my leave. I was not christened of my own will. My parents had me christened before I knew any thing about it! I had no choice!"

Is it so? Do you know what your words mean? If they mean anything, they mean that you had rather not have been christened, because you are now expected to behave as a christened man should. Now is there any one of you who dare say, "I wish I had not been christened?"

Not one! Then if you dare not say that; if you are content to have been christened, why are you not content to do what christened people should? If you are content to have been christened, you are christened people now of your own free will, and are bound to act accordingly.

But why were you christened? not merely because your parents chose, but because it was their duty. Every child ought to be christened, because every child belongs to Christ. Every child is in debt to Christ,—every child is bound to serve Christ.

In debt to Christ, you say? Certainly, from the moment you are born, and before that too. You are in debt to Him since you were born, for every good thought and feeling which ever came into your hearts and minds, for He put them there. And will any of you answer, "Then I wish He had not put them there, if they are to bring me into debt to Him, and force me to serve Him. I don't wish, of course, that I had been bad; but I wish that I had been neither good nor bad. I wish I had had no immortal soul, which is bound to serve Christ."

Now does any man of you wish that really? Dare any of you wish that you were like the beasts, without conscience, without honour, without shame, without knowing right from wrong, without any life after death, without being able even to talk—for mind, without immortal souls men could not speak. The beasts cannot talk to each other; reasonable speech belongs to our souls, not to our bodies. Then if you are glad that you have souls, and are better than the dumb beasts, you confess that you feel in debt to Christ, and are bound to serve Him. For who gave you your souls but Christ?

But even if you had had no souls, you would have been in debt to Christ, and bound to serve Him. "What for?" you ask. Why, for life itself. How did you come here? Who gave you life? Who brought you into the world? Who but Christ, by whom all things were made, and you among the rest? Who gave you food? Who made every atom of food grow which you ate since you were born?

Who made the air you breathe, the water which you drink, the wool and cotton which clothes you? Who but Christ? Do you not know that you cannot even breathe a breath of air, unless Christ first makes the air, and then gives your lungs life to breathe the air? and yet you cannot understand that you are in debt to Christ, and have been eating His bread and living on His bounty ever since you were born?

And mind, all this while I have not said one word about the greatest debt of all which you owe to the Lord Jesus Christ, even His own life, which He gave for you! Only think but once that for your sakes the Lord was crucified—for your sakes He died the most horrible, painful, shameful death. And then say, Are you not in debt to Him? "Greater love has no man than this, that he lay down his life for his friends." If any mere man had died for your sake, would you not love him—would you not feel yourself in debt to him, a deeper debt than you can ever repay? Then Christ died for you—how can you be more deeply in debt to any one than to Him?

You have now no right to choose between Christ and the devil, because Christ has chosen you already—no right to choose between good and bad, because God, the good God Himself, has chosen you already, and has been taking care of you, and heaping you with blessings ever since you were born.

And why did Christ choose you? As I have told you, that you may fight with Him against all that is bad. Jesus Christ's work at which He works for ever in heaven and in earth, is to root out all that is bad, all sin, all misery; and He will reign, and He will fight till all His enemies, even Death itself, are put under His feet and destroyed. And Christ expects you and me to help Him. He has chosen you and me, and all Christian people, to fight against what is bad, and to put it down and root it out as far as we can wherever we find it; and therefore, first, to root it out of our own hearts and lives; for while we are bad ourselves we cannot make others good. But if we go on doing bad and wrong things, are we fighting on Christ's side? No, we are fighting on the devil's side, and helping the devil against God.

Do you fancy that I am saying too much? I suspect some do. I suspect some say in their hearts, "He is too hard on us. We are not like that traitorous soldier. If an English soldier went over to the enemy, and fought against the English, and killed Englishmen, that of course would be too bad; but we do not wish to harm any one, much less our neighbours. If we do wrong, it is ourselves at most that we harm. If we do wrong, it is only we that shall suffer for it. Why does he talk as if we were robbers or murderers, or had a spite against our neighbours? We do not wish to hurt any one, we do not want to help the devil."

Now, my friends, if any of you say that, do you not say first what is not true? and next do you not know that it is not true?

First, It is not true that by doing wrong you hurt no one but yourself. Every wrong thing which any man does, every wrong way into which he runs, is certain sooner or later to hurt his neighbours. The worse man a man is, the worse for those who have to do with him. You know it is your own case. You know that bad people hurt you, and make you unhappy; and that good people do you good and make you happy. You know that bad example does you harm and good example does you good. Think for yourselves—use your own common sense. Recollect what you know, what has happened to you again and again. You know that if any one uses bad language before you, you are tempted to use bad language too. If any one quarrels with you, you are tempted to quarrel with him. You know that if parents do wrong things before their children, the children learn to copy them. It is nonsense to talk of a man keeping his sins to himself. No man does, and no man can. Out of the abundance of a man's heart his mouth speaks; and a bad tree will bring forth bad fruit. If there are bad thoughts in your head, they will come out in bad words. If there are bad tempers in your heart, they will come out in bad and unkind and dishonest actions. You may as well try to keep in fire, as to keep in sin. It will break out, and it will burn whatever it touches. And if you, or I, or any one does wrong in any thing, we shall surely hurt some one or other by it. If you, or I, or any one is worse than he ought to be, we shall make the parish we live in worse than it ought to be. You know that it is so. Who made you different from the rest of the world? If any body else's sins are harmful, who will make your sins harmless? Not the devil, for he wishes to see as much harm done as possible. And not God, for He will not be so cruel as to let your sin prosper and go unpunished, as it would if it did not make people hate it, by feeling the bad effects of it.

My good friends, if you by doing wrong hurt other people, and make other people unhappy, are you doing Christ's work or the devil's? Are you fighting for Christ, who wishes to make all good, or for the devil, who wishes to make all bad? Are you Christ's faithful soldier and servant, or are you a traitor to Christ who has gone over to the devil's side, and is helping the devil to make this poor world (which is bad enough already) worse than it is?

Oh, think of this now, while you have time before you. Remember all that Christ has done for you, and remember that all He asks of you in return is to do for Him nothing but good, which is good for you as well as for your neighbours. The devil's wages now are shame, discontent, unhappiness, perhaps poverty, perhaps sickness, certainly punishment as traitors to Christ after we die. Christ's wages are love, joy, peace, the answer of a good conscience, the respect and love of all good men, as long as we live, and after death, life everlasting. Choose; will you be traitors or deserters, and serve the worst of all masters, the King of Hell, or be honest, honourable, and brave men, and serve the best of all masters, the King of Heaven, the Lord of Life, and love, and goodness without bound, whose ways are ways of pleasantness, and all His paths are peace?

XXIV

HOLY COMMUNION;

CHRIST AND THE SINNER

"Have mercy upon, me, O God, according to thy loving-kindness; according unto the multitude of thy tender mercies blot out my transgressions. Wash me thoroughly from mine iniquity, and cleanse me from my sin. For I acknowledge my transgressions: and my sin is ever before me. The sacrifices of God are a broken spirit: a broken and a contrite heart, O God, thou wilt not despise."—Psalm li. 1, 2, 3, 17.

This Psalm was written by David when he was sorrowing for sin, and if there are any such among you, my dear friends, let me speak a few words to you. Would to God that I had the tongue of St. Paul to speak to you with—though even when he preached some mocked, as it will be to the end. But if to one of you God has brought home His truth, then to that one conscience-stricken sinner I will say, "You confess with David that all your sorrows are your own fault. Thank God that He has taught you so much."

But what will you do to be saved from your sins? "I cannot wait," you say in your heart, "to go home and begin leading a new life. I will do that, please God, but I want to know at once that I am forgiven. I want to be saved. I cannot save myself. I cannot save myself from hell hereafter, or from this miserable sinful life, nearly as bad as hell here. Oh! wretched being that I am, who shall deliver me from the body of this death?"

Friend, dost thou not know it is written, "Believe in the Lord Jesus Christ, and thou shalt be saved."

"Ah yes!" says the sinner, "I have been hearing that all my life, and much good it has done me! Look at me, I want something more than those words about Christ, I want Christ Himself to save me if He can."

Ah, my brother!—poor sinner! thou hast never believed in Christ, thou hast only believed about Christ. There was the fault. But Christ Himself will save thee, though thou hast been the worst of reprobates, He will save thee. Only one thing, He will have thee answer first. "Dost thou wish to be saved from the punishment of thy sins, or from the sins themselves?"

"From my sins—from my sins," says the man who truly repents. "They are what I hate, even while I commit them. I hate and despise myself, I dare look neither God nor man in the face, and yet I go on doing the very things I loathe the next minute. Oh, for some one to save me from my own ill-temper, my own bitter tongue, my own laziness, my own canting habits, my own dishonesty, my own lustfulness. But who will save me from them? who will change me and make a new creature of me? Oh, for a sign from heaven that I can get rid of these bad habits! I hate them, and yet I love them. I long to give them up, and yet, if some one stronger than me does not have mercy on me, I shall go and do them again to-morrow. I am longing to do wrong now, and yet I long not to do wrong. Oh, for a sign from heaven!"

Poor sinner!—My brother! there is a sign from heaven for thee! On that table it stands. A sign that Christ's blood was shed to wash out thy sins, a sign that Christ's blood will feed thee, and give thy spirit strength to cast away and hate thy sins. Come to Holy Communion and claim thy share in Christ's pardon for the past, in Christ's strength for the future.

"What!" says the sinner, "I come to the Sacrament! I of all men the most unfit! I who but yesterday committed such and such sins!"

Friend, as to the sin you committed yesterday, confess that to God, not me. And if you confess it to Him, He is faithful and just to forgive it. But just because you think yourself the most unfit person to come to the Holy Sacrament, for that very reason I suspect you to be fit.

"How then!" says he in his heart, "I have but this moment repented of my sins! I have but this moment, for the first time felt that God's wrath is revealed against me, that hell is open for me!"

For that very reason, come to the Holy Sacrament, and thou shalt hear there that not hell at all, but heaven is open for thee.

"What, with all this guilty conscience, this load of sins against myself, my neighbours, my children, my masters, my servants, on my back!"

Yes, bring them all, and say in the words of the Communion Service: "I do earnestly repent, and am heartily sorry for these, my misdoings; the remembrance of them is grievous unto me; the burden of them is intolerable." Why, for whom were these words written, but for you who feel that the burden of your sins is intolerable. They are there, not for those who feel no burden of sin, but for you—for you, and for those like you who feel the burden of your sins unbearable.

"But how shall I dare to come to the Lord's table before I am sure that my sins are forgiven?"

Come and you will hear your minister pray God to pardon and deliver you from all for Christ's sake. You will hear him read God's promises of free grace and mercy through Jesus Christ to all who truly repent.

"But I cannot trust your prayers or words, or any man's. I want a sign that I have a share in Christ's death and merits."

Then, that bread and wine is a sign. Jesus Himself ordained them for a sign. He Himself, with His dying voice declared that that bread was His body, that cup the new covenant in His blood. St. Paul declares that it is the communion, the sharing of Christ's body, that cup the sharing of His blood. What more sign do you want? Come and claim your share in Christ, and see if He disappoints you.

"Ah! I believe," says the poor man, "I believe, but I am afraid, afraid of partaking unworthily, and so provoking God, as the Prayer-book says to plague me with divers diseases and sundry kinds of death."

My Friend, if God was the devil, you might be afraid indeed. But He is the loving, righteous Father, who knows your weakness, and remembers that you are but dust. Can you not trust Him to pardon your mistakes about the Sacrament, which you do not wilfully intend to commit, when He has borne with, and pardoned all the sins from your youth up until now, which you have wilfully committed? Surely, you may trust Him in such a thing as this,—He who has had long-suffering enough to keep you alive, with a chance of salvation all this time? and as for sundry diseases, have you avoided them? You have certainly not avoided them, at least, by staying away from the Sacrament, and breaking Christ's command to take it? If you are so afraid of God's anger, are you more likely to provoke Him by disobeying His strict commands, or by obeying them? It needs no philosopher, my friend, to find out that.

"But I shall have to make good resolutions," says the sinner, "and I am afraid of breaking them."

Well, if you break them, you can but make them again. You would call him a fool who determined never to walk, because he was afraid of falling. But you are to claim in that Sacrament your share of Christ's Spirit, Christ's life, and Christ's strength, which is just what you want to enable you to keep your good resolutions. You will be no stronger, no more righteous of yourself after the Sacrament than before. Your spirit will still be a poor weak sinful spirit, but you will have claimed your share in God's strength, God's righteousness, God's Spirit, and they will make you love the good you hated, and hate the evil you loved. They will make you strong to do God's will whatever it may cost you. Oh believe the good news, and show that you believe by coming to Christ. He, the Blessed One, died for you. For you He was born and walked this earth, a poor suffering, tempted, sorrow-stricken man. For you He hung upon the shameful cross. For you He ascended up on high. For you He sent down His Spirit. For you He sits at the right hand of God, praying for you at this moment. For you He gave the signs of His body and His blood, that you might believe, and fall on your knees and cry, "In spite of all, I am forgiven. In spite of all, God cares for me. In spite of all, I have a Father and a Saviour who will never leave me, nor forsake me, wretch as I have been, till they make a man of me again, in this world, and for ever!" Oh! come, my dear, dear friends. I would give my right hand this moment, if I could but see each and every one of you shewing the truth of your repentance by coming to Holy Communion. Let this be a day of repentance, and shew it thus, and say, "We do not come to this, Thy table, O Lord, trusting in our own righteousness, but in Thy manifold and great mercy. We are not worthy to gather up the crumbs under Thy table, but Thou art the same Lord whose property is always to have mercy."

Let this be a day of thanksgiving, too, and shew your thankfulness by coming to Holy Communion, and lifting up your voices, once for all, at that table, and saying:—

"We bless Thee, we praise Thee, we glorify Thee, we give thanks to Thee for Thy great glory." These are the words for you this day. Oh! do not turn away. All your distress, all your sorrows have come from your not having faith in God. Break at once the accursed charm with which the devil has enchanted you. Have faith enough to come to God's holy table, and see if God does not reward you by giving you faith enough to conquer yourselves, and lead new lives like redeemed men in the sunshine of His smile, henceforth and forever!

My friends, what more can I say, except once and again, Come ye who labour and are heavy laden, and Christ will give you rest!

Ay, and He will. I speak only what I know—what I have felt. But before He will give you rest, be you rich or poor, young or old, you must learn to say those simple words (they are the best and only preparation for it), "God be merciful to me a sinner." Say them then from your heart, and so come to the Lord's Supper.

A PRAYER

"O God and Saviour, Thou hast blest me, and I have cursed myself. Thou didst die to deliver me from the curse of sin, and I have brought it back on myself by my own folly. Thou livest for ever to make me good, and I, ungrateful and foolish, have made myself bad. In spite of my ingratitude, in spite of my folly, take me back into Thy service. I trust utterly in Thy unchangeable goodness and mercy. I trust that Thy blood will still wash away the past, that Thy spirit will still give me a clean heart and a right spirit. I believe that though I have cursed myself, yet Thou wilt still bless me; for Thou wiliest nought but the good of every creature Thou hast made. God be merciful to me a sinner!" Amen.

PART II

I

BRAVE WORDS FOR BRAVE SOLDIERS AND SAILORS[3]

My friends,—I speak to you simply as brave men. I speak alike to Roman Catholic and Protestant. I speak alike to godly men and ungodly. I speak alike to soldiers and sailors.... If you are brave, read these words. I call these brave words. They are not my own words, or my own message, but the message to you of the bravest man who ever lived, or who ever will live, and if you will read them and think over them, He will not make you brave (for that, thank God, you are already), but keep you brave, come victory or defeat. I speak to the brave men who have now fought three bloody battles, and fought them like heroes. All England has blessed you, and admired you; all England has felt for you in a way that would do your hearts good to see. For you know as well as I, that nothing is so comforting, nothing so endearing, as sympathy, as to know that people feel for one. If one knows that, one can dare and do anything. If one feels that nobody cares for one's suffering or one's success, one is ready to lie down and die. It is so with a horse or a dog even. If there is any noble spirit in them, a word of encouragement will make them go till they drop. How much more will the spirit of a man? I can well believe that the Queen's beautiful letter put more heart into you, than the hope of all the prize money in the world would have done; and that with the words of that letter ringing in your ears, you will prove true to the last, to the words of the grand old song—

> "Hearts of oak are our ships, hearts of oak are our men,
> And we'll fight, and we'll conquer again, and again."

But, my friends, you know as well as I, that there are times when neither that letter, nor the feeling of duty, nor of honour, nor of glory, can keep your hearts from sinking. Not in battle! No. Only cowards' hearts fail them there; and there are no cowards among you. But even a brave man's heart may fail him at whiles,

---

[3] This was written and sent out to the army before Sebastopol in the winter of 1855.

when, instead of the enemy's balls and bayonets, he has to face delay, and disappointment, and fatigue, and sickness, and hunger, and cold, and nakedness; as you have, my brave brothers, and faced them as well as man ever did on earth. Ah! it must be fearful work to sit still, and shiver and starve in a foreign land, and to think of those who are in comfort and plenty at home; and worse, to think of those, who, even if they are in plenty, cannot be in comfort, because their hearts are breaking for your sake; to think of brother and sister, wife and child, while you are pacing up and down those dreary trenches, waiting for your turn of sickness, perhaps of death. It must be bitter and disheartening at times; you would not be men, if it was not. One minute, perhaps, you remember that those whom you have left at home, love you and pray for you; and that cheers you; then you remember that all England loves you, and prays for you in every church throughout the land; and that cheers you; but even that is not enough, you feel ready to say, "What is the use of my going through all this misery? Why am I not at home ploughing the ground, or keeping a shop, anything rather than throwing away my life by inches thus. My people at home feel for me, but they cannot know, they never will know, the half of what I have gone through. The nation will provide for me if I am crippled, but they cannot make up to me for losing the best years of my life in such work as this; and, if I am killed, can they make up to me for that? Who can make up to me for my life?"

Have you not had such thoughts, my friends, and sadder thoughts still lately? You need not be ashamed of them if you have. For hard work you have had, and it must have told at times on your spirits as heavily as it has on your bodies.

But, my friends, there is an answer for these sad thoughts. There are brave words for you, and a noble message from God, which will cheer you when nothing else can cheer you. If your own people cannot know all that you go through, there is One who can and does; if your own wives and mothers cannot feel enough for you, there is One above who does, and He is the Lord Jesus Christ. You have hungered; so has He. You have been weary; so has He. You have felt cold and nakedness; so has He. You have been houseless and sleepless, so has He. While the foxes had holes, and the birds of the air had nests, He, the maker of them all, had not where to lay His head. You have felt the misery of loneliness and desolation; but never so much as did He, when not only every earthly friend forsook Him and fled, but He cried out in His very death pangs, "My God, my God, why hast Thou forsaken me?"

Above all, you have felt how difficult it was to die, not fighting sword in hand, but slowly and idly, and helplessly, by cholera or fever, hunger or cold. Terrible it is; but the Lord Jesus Christ has felt that too. For three years He looked death in the face—a death of shame and misery such as you can never die—and faced it, and gave Himself up to it of His own free will; and though He had the most horrible fear of it to the very last, He determined to submit to it, in spite of His own fear of it; and He did submit to it, and died, and so showed, even in His very fear, the most perfect and glorious courage. So if any one of you has ever felt for a single moment afraid; even in that, the Lord Jesus Christ can feel for you; for He, too, has gone through the agony of fear, when His sweat was as great drops of blood falling to the ground, that He might be able to help you, and every man that is tempted, because He can be touched with the feeling of your infirmities, having gone through every temptation which flesh is heir to, and conquered them all.

This, then, is one half (and only one half) of my good news; that you have a Friend in heaven who feels for every trouble of yours, better than your own mothers can feel for you, because He has been through it all already; you have a Friend in heaven who is praying for you day and night, more earnestly, lovingly, wisely, than your own wives and children are praying for you. But that is not all. God forbid! You have a Friend in heaven, for whose sake God will forgive you all your sins and weaknesses, as often as you heartily confess them to Him, and trust in Him for a full and free pardon. You have a Friend in heaven who will help you day by day, where you most need help, in your hearts and spirits; who will give you, if you ask Him, His Spirit, the same spirit of duty, courage, endurance, love, self-sacrifice, which made Him brave to endure ten thousand times more than any soldier or sailor can endure, for the sake of doing His Father's will, and saving a ruined world.

Oh! open your hearts to Him, my brave men, in your lonely night-watches—on your sick beds; ay, in the very roar of battle itself, ask Him to make you true and good, patient, calm, prudent, honourable, obedient, gentle, even in the hottest of the fight. Commit to Him your own lives and fortunes, and the lives and fortunes of those who have been left at home, and be sure that He, your Unseen Friend of friends, is able and willing to help to the uttermost all that you put into His charge.

But, again, my men, if the nation cannot reward you for sacrificing your life in a just war, there is One above who can, and who will, too; for He is as just as He is loving, and as loving as He is just, and that is the same of whom I have spoken already, the Lord Jesus Christ.

I think some of you will fancy this almost too good news to be true, and yet the very news which you want to hear. I think some of you have been saying as you read this, "All this is blessed and comforting news for poor fellows lying wounded in a hospital, or fretting their souls away about the wives and children they have left behind; blessed and comforting news; but we want something more than that even. We have to fight and to kill; we want to be sure that God's blessing is on our fighting and our killing; we have to go into battle; and we want to know that there, too, we are doing God's work, and to be sure that God is on our side."

Well, my brave men, Be sure of it then! Be sure that God's blessing is as much upon you; be sure that you are doing God's work, as much when you are handling a musket or laying a gun in your country's battles, as when you are bearing frost and hunger in the trenches, and pain and weakness on a sick bed.

For the Lord Jesus Christ is not only the Prince of Peace; He is the Prince of War too. He is the Lord of Hosts, the God of armies; and whosoever fights in a just war, against tyrants and oppressors, he is fighting on Christ's side, and Christ is fighting on his side; Christ is his Captain and his Leader, and he can be in no better service. Be sure of it; for the Bible tells you so. The old wars of Abraham against the robber-kings; of Joshua against the Canaanites; of David against the Philistines; of Hezekiah against the Assyrians; of the Maccabees against the Greeks—all tell the soldier the same brave news, that he is doing God's work, and that God's blessing is on him, when he fights in a just cause. And you are fighting in a just cause, if you are fighting for freedom and law. If to you God gives the noble work of fighting for the liberty of Europe, God will reward you according as you do that work like men. You will be fighting in that everlasting war which is in heaven; in God's everlasting war against all injustice and wrong, the Captain and Leader whereof is the Lord Jesus Christ Himself. Believe that—for the Bible tells it you. You must think of the Lord Jesus Christ, not merely as a sufferer, but as a warrior; not merely as the Man of Sorrows (blessed as that thought is), but as the Lord of Hosts—the God of armies—the King who executes justice and judgment in the earth, who has sworn vengeance against all unrighteousness and wrong, and will destroy the wicked with the breath of His mouth. You must think of Him as the God of the fatherless and the widow; but you must think of Him, too, as the God of the sailor and the soldier, the God of duty, the God of justice, the God of vengeance, the God to whom your colours were solemnly offered, and His blessing on them prayed for, when they were given to your regiment.

I know that you would follow those colours into the mouth of the pit, that you would die twice over sooner than let them be taken.

Good! but remember, too, that those colours are a sign to you that Christ is with you, ready to give you courage, coolness, and right judgment, in the charge and in the death grapple, just as much as He is with those ministering angels who will nurse and tend your wounds in hospital. God's blessing is on them; but do you never forget that your colours are a sign to you that Christ's blessing is on you. If they do not mean that to you, what was the use of blessing them with prayer? It must have been a lie and a sham. But it is no lie, brave men, and no sham; it is a glorious truth, of which those noble rags, inscribed with noble names of victory, should remind you every day and every hour, that he who fights for Queen and country in a just cause, is fighting not only in the Queen's army, but in Christ's army, and that he shall in no wise lose his reward.

Are not these brave words for brave soldiers? Well: they are not mine; they are the Bible's. The book of Revelation tells us how St. John saw a vision of the Lord Jesus Christ, and of His everlasting war against wrong, of which I spoke just now. And what did the Lord appear like?

"And I saw heaven opened, and behold a white horse; and he that sat upon him is called Faithful and True, and in righteousness He doth judge and make war. And His eyes were as a flame of fire; and He was clothed in a garment dipped in blood; and His name is called the Word of God. And the armies in heaven followed Him, riding upon white horses, clothed in fine linen, white and clean. And out of His mouth goeth a sharp sword, that He should smite the nations; and He shall rule them with a rod of iron; and He treadeth the winepress of the fierceness and of the wrath of almighty God" (Rev. xix. 11).

Are not these brave words, my friends? Are not these soldier-like words? Is not this a general worth following? Is not this a charge of cavalry worth sharing in? Then believe that that general, the Lord Jesus Christ, is your general. Believe that you are sharing in that everlasting charge, to which the glorious charge of Balaclava was as nothing; the everlasting war which the Lord Jesus wages against all sin, and cruelty, and wrong—in which He will never draw bridle-rein, or sheath His sword, till He has put all enemies under His feet, and swept all oppression, injustice, and wickedness off the face of the earth which God has given Him.

Therefore I can say to you other brave words, my friends (and not my own, but the words of the same Lord Jesus Christ):—"Fear not them that can kill the body, and after that have no more that they can do. But I will forewarn you whom you shall fear; fear him who after he has killed has power to destroy both body and soul in hell."

Now all England knows already that you do not fear those who can kill the body; but I sometimes fear that some of you are not enough afraid of that enemy worst of all, who can kill the soul too. And who is that? St. Paul tells us. He is "the devil, who has the power of death," who lies in ambuscade to destroy your body and soul in hell; and will and can do it; but only if you let him. Now who is the devil? It is worth your while to know; for many a man may be, as you are, in the ranks of God's army, and yet doing the devil's work all the while. Many a man may fancy himself a good soldier, and forget that a soldier is a man, and something more; and that therefore, before you can be a good soldier, you must first be more or less of a good man. Do you think not? Look then, and see whether the most upright and god-fearing men in your ranks are not in the long run the best soldiers. I don't mean merely the best fighters—the bravest men in battle. There goes more than mere bull-dog pluck to the making of a soldier; and to make a good soldier, I hold that a man, though he be afraid of nothing else, must be horribly afraid of the devil, and that the better and braver soldier he is, the more afraid of the devil he will be.

Of course that depends upon who the devil is. I will tell you. He is what his name means, the accuser and the divider—the evil spirit who sets men against each other—men against officers, and officers against men; who sets men grumbling, puts hard suspicious thoughts into their minds; makes them selfish and forgetful of their duty, tempts them to care only for themselves, and help themselves. You must see that if those tempers once got head in an army, there would be an end of all discipline—of all obedience; and what is more, of all courage; for if the devil could completely persuade every man to care only for himself, the plain thing for every man to do, would be to turn round and run for his life. That you will never do; but you may give way to the devil in lesser matters, and so do God's work ill, and lose your own reward from God. All grumbling, and hard speeches, and tale-bearing is doing the devil's work. All disorder and laziness is doing the devil's work. All cruelty and brutality is doing the devil's work.

Now as to cruelty and brutality, some soldiers fancy when towns are taken in war, that they may do things for which (to speak the truth) they ought to be hanged. I mean in plain English, ravishing the women, and ill-treating unarmed men, to make them give up their money. Whosoever does these things, God's curse is on him, and his sin will surely find him out. No excuse of being in hot blood will avail him. No excuse of having fought well beforehand will avail him. Such cant will no more excuse him with God than it will with truly noble-minded men. He may have been brave enough before, but he is doing a coward's deed then; he is doing the devil's work, and the devil, and not God, will pay him his wages, to the uttermost farthing. But though I tell you to fear the devil, it is only to fear his getting the command over you. The devil is a liar, and a liar is always a coward. Be brave in God's service. "Resist the devil and he will flee from you."

One word more. If any of you are maddened by hearing of the enemy murdering some of your wounded—recollect that revenge is one of the devil's works, of which the brave men cannot be too much afraid. God forbid that you should ever be maddened into imitating such cruelty. Fight the enemy in God's name—and strike home; but never have on your conscience the thought that you struck an unnecessary blow. You are to kill for the sake of victory, but never to kill for the sake of killing. You know who it was who prayed for and excused His own murderers as He hung upon the cross. "Father, forgive them, for they know not what they do." That was the same Lord Jesus who, as I told you, is the great Warrior against all wrong. If He was not ashamed to forgive, do you not be ashamed either. You cannot be more brave than He is; try, at least, to be merciful like Him. Overcome evil with good; by returning good for evil you will not only help England's cause by softening the hearts of your enemies, but you will preach Christ's gospel to them—and in nowise lose your reward.

Remember then, always, our Lord Jesus Christ is the pattern of a perfect warrior, whether by land or sea; and if you be like Him, and fighting not only on His side, but as He likes to see you fight, that is, righteously and mercifully against the tyrants of the earth—what harm can happen to you? Be sure that whether you live, you will live to Him; or whether you die, you die to Him; that living or dying you will be His; and that He is merciful (the Bible says) in this, that He rewards every man according to his work. Do you your work like men, and be sure that the Lord Jesus Christ will see that you are right well paid, if not in this life, still in that life to come, to which may He bring you and all brave men, who will strive to do their duty in that station of life to which God has called them.

II

THE STORY OF CORTEZ; OR PLUCK IN THE SIXTEENTH CENTURY.

A LECTURE DELIVERED AT ALDERSHOT CAMP, NOV. 1858

It seemed to me that, having to speak to-night to soldiers, that I ought to speak about soldiers. Some story, I thought, about your own profession would please you most and teach you most. Some story, I say, for it is not my business to tell you what soldiers ought to be like. That, I daresay, you know a great deal better than I; and I only hope I may do my duty as a parson half as well as British soldiers do their duty, and will always do it.

So I thought of telling you to-night some sort of a story—a true one, of course, about wars and battles—some story about the British army; but then I thought there are plenty of officers who can do that far better than I,—so I will take some story of foreign armies, and one of old times too. And though no soldier myself, but only a scholar, and reader of queer old books, I may make my scholarship of some use to you who have to drill and fight, and die too, for us comfortable folks who sit at home and read our books by our fireside.

Then I thought of the story of Cortez the Spaniard, and how he conquered the great empire of Mexico with a handful of brave men. That, I thought, would be an example to you of what men can do who have stout hearts and good weapons, and who have faith too in God, and believe that if they do their duty God will prosper them. And I thought I could do it all the better, because I like the story, and enjoy reading it again and again; for I know no such dashing and desperate deed of courage in history, except Havelock's advance upon Lucknow.

So now I will begin my story, telling you first where Mexico is, and what it was like when Cortez landed in it, more than three hundred years ago.

You, all of you, have heard of the West India station—some of you have been there. Beyond those West India Islands lies the great Gulf of Mexico, and beyond that the mainland of North America, and Mexico itself. It is now thinly peopled by Spaniards, the descendants of settlers who came over after Cortez's time; and a very lazy, cowardly set most of them are,—very different from the old heroes, their forefathers. Our Yankee cousins can lick them now, one to five, and will end, I believe, in conquering the whole country. But in Cortez's time, the place was very different. It was full of vast numbers of heathens, brownish coloured people, something like the Red Indians you see in Canada, but a fairer, handsomer, stouter, heavier-bodied race; and much more civilised also. They had great cities and idol temples, aqueducts for water, and all sorts of noble buildings, all of most curiously carved stone; which is all the more wonderful and creditable to them, when we remember that they had no iron—not a knife—not a nail of iron among them. But they had found out how to make bronze by mixing tin and copper, and with it could work the hardest stones, as well as we can with iron. They had another stuff which was curious enough, of which they made knives, razors, arrow heads, and saw-edged swords as keen as razors—and that was glass. They did not make the glass—they found it about the burning mountains, of which Mexico is full; itztli they called it; we call it obsidian. It is tougher than our glass, and chips to a fine razor edge. I have seen arrows of it, which I am certain would go clean through a man, and knives which would take his arm off, bone and all. I want you to remember these glass weapons, for Cortez's Spaniards had cause enough to remember them when they came to fight. Gunpowder, of course, they knew nothing of, nor of horses or cattle either. They had no beasts of draught; and all the stones and timber for their magnificent buildings were carried by hand. But they were first-rate farmers; and for handicraft work, such as pottery, weaving, and making all kinds of ornaments, I can answer for it, for I have seen a good deal of their work—they had not then their equals in the world. They made the most beautiful dresses out of the feathers of birds—parrots, humming birds, and such like, which fill the forests in hot countries. And what was more, their country abounded in gold and jewels, and they knew how to work them, just as well as we do. They could work gold into the likeness of flowers, of birds with every feather like life, and into a thousand trinkets. Their soil was most fruitful of all that man can want—there was enough of the best for all to eat; and altogether there never was a richer, and need never have been a happier people, if they had but been good. But that was just what they were not. A bad lot they were, cruel and blood-thirsty, continually at war with each other; and as for cruelty, just take this one story. At the opening of a great temple to one of their idols in 1486, about thirty years before the Spaniards came, they sacrificed to the idol seventy-thousand human beings!

This offering in sacrifice of human beings to their idols was their regular practice. They got these poor creatures by conquering all the nations round, and carrying back their prisoners to sacrifice; and if they failed, they took poor people of their own, for blood they and their false gods must have. Men, and sometimes women and children, were murdered by them in their temples, often with the most horrible tortures, to the number, I am afraid there is no doubt of it, of many thousands every year; and their flesh afterwards cooked delicately, was eaten as a luxury by people who, as far as outward show went, were just as fine gentlemen and ladies as there are now.

When the Spaniards got into Mexico, they found the walls of the temples crusted inches thick in blood, the altars of the idols heaped with smoking human hearts, and whole houses full of skulls. They counted in one house one hundred and thirty-six thousand skulls. It was high time to get rid of those Mexicans off the face of the earth; and in God's good time a man was found to rid the earth of them, and that man was Hernando Cortez.

And who was Cortez? He was a poor young Spanish gentleman, son of an infantry captain, who, in his youth, was sickly and weakly; and his father tried to make a lawyer of him, and would have done it, but young Cortez kicked over the traces, as we say, right and left, and turned out such a wild fellow, that he would not stay at college; and after getting into plenty of scrapes, started as a soldier to the West Indies when he was only nineteen. Little did people think what stuff there was in that wild, sickly lad!

How he got on in the Spanish West Indies would be a long story. I will only tell you that he turned out a thoroughly good soldier, and a very dashing smart fellow, a first-rate rider and fencer, a great dandy in his dress; but also—and if you go to hot climates, keep this in mind—a particularly sober and temperate man, who drank nothing, and could eat anything. And he had, it is said, the most extraordinary power of managing his men. He was always cool and determined; and what he said had to be done, and they knew it; but his way with them was so frank and kind, and he was so ready to be the foremost in daring and enduring, living worse often than his own men, while he was doing every thing for their comfort, that there was nothing they would not do for him, as the event proved—for if those soldiers had not trusted him for life and death, I should not have this grand story to tell.

At last he married a very pretty woman, and got an estate in the West Indies, and settled down there; and the chances were ten to one that no one ever heard of him. However, dim reports came to the West Indies of this great empire of Mexico, and of all its wonders and wealth, and that stirred up Cortez's blood; and nothing would serve him but that leaving wife and estate, he must start out again to seek his fortune.

He got a commission from the Governor, such as it was, for they were lawless places those Spanish West Indies then; and everybody fulfilled a certain Irishman's notion of true liberty—for he did "what was right in the sight of his own eyes, and what was wrong too"—and Cortez's commission was to go and discover this country, and trade with the people, and make Christians of them—that is, if he could.

So he got together a little army, and sailed away with it for the unknown land. He had about one hundred sailors, five hundred and fifty soldiers armed with sword and pike, and among them thirty-two cross-bow men, and thirteen musketeers. Above all, he had sixteen horses, ten heavy guns—or what may be called heavy guns in those times—about 9-pounders, I suppose, and four smaller guns; and with that he set out to conquer a new world; and he conquered it!

He did not know whither he was going. All he knew was, that this wonderful country of Mexico was somewhere, and treasures inestimable in it. And one other thing he knew, that if mortal man could get there, he would.

He landed at Tabasco—where Vera Cruz city stands now—fought with the Indians, who ran away at the sight of the horses and noise of the cannon; and then made friends with them. From them he got presents, and among others, a present which was worth more than its weight in gold to him, namely, a young slave girl, who had been born near Mexico, and knew the language. She was very clever, and very beautiful; and soon learnt to speak Spanish. She had been a princess in her own country, and was sold as a slave by her cruel stepmother. They made a Christian of her, and called her Dona Marina,—her Indian name was Malinche,—and she became Cortez's interpreter to the Indians, and his secretary. And she loved him and served him as faithfully as true woman ever loved man, and saved him and his from a hundred dangers. And the Spaniards reverence her name still; and call a mighty snow mountain after her, Malinche, to this day.

After that he marched inland, hearing more and more of the wonders of Mexico, till he came at last, after many adventures, to a country called Tlascala, up among high mountains.

The men who lived there seem to have been rough honest fellows; and brave enough they showed themselves. The Mexicans who lived in the plains below never could conquer them, though they had been fighting with them for full two hundred years. These Tlascalans turned out like men, and fought Cortez—one hundred Indians to one Spaniard they fought for four mortal hours; but horses and cannon were too much for them, and by evening they were beaten off. They attempted to surprise him the same night, and were beaten off again with great slaughter. Whereon a strange thing happened.

Cortez, through Dona Marina, his interpreter, sent them in fair terms. If they would make peace he would forget and forgive all; if not, he would kill every man of them, and level their city to the ground. Whereon, after more fighting, the Tlascalans behaved like wise and brave men. They understood at last that Cortez's point was not Tlascala, but Mexico; and the Mexicans were their bitterest enemies; and they had the good sense to shake hands with the Spaniards, and make all up. And faithful friends they were, and bravely they fought side by side during all the terrible campaign that followed. Meanwhile, Cortez's own men began to lose heart. They had had terrible fighting already, and no plunder. As for getting to Mexico, it was all a dream. But Cortez and Dona Marina, this wonderful Indian girl, kept them up. No doubt they were in awful danger—a handful of strangers walking blindfold in a vast empire, not one foot of ground of which they knew: but Cortez knew the further they went the further they must go, for it was impossible to go back. So on and on they went; and as they went they met ambassadors from Montezuma, the great Emperor of Mexico. The very sight of these men confirmed all that they had heard of the riches of that great empire, for these Indian lords came blazing with gold and jewels, and the most magnificent dresses; and of their power, for at one city which had let Cortez in peaceably without asking the Emperor's leave, they demanded as a fine five and twenty Indian young men and forty girls to be offered in sacrifice to their idols. Cortez answered that by clapping them in irons, and then sending them back to the Emperor, with a message that whether he liked or not, he was coming to Mexico.

You may call that desperate rashness; but like a good deal of rashness, it paid. This great Emperor Montezuma was utterly panic-stricken. There were old prophecies that white gods should come over the sea and destroy him and his empire; and he took it into his head that these Spaniards were the white gods, and that there was no use resisting them. He had been a brave man in his youth, and a great warrior; but he utterly lost his head now. He sent magnificent presents to the Spaniards to buy them off; but that only made them the more keen to come on; and come they did, till they saw underneath them the city of Mexico, which must have been then one of the wonders of the world.

It lay in the midst of a great salt lake, and could only be reached from shore by long causeways, beautifully built of stone. On this lake were many islands; and what was most curious of all, floating gardens, covered with all sorts of vegetables and flowers.

How big the city was no one will ever know now; but the old ruins of it show how magnificent its buildings must have been, full of palaces and temples of every kind of carved stone, surrounded by flower gardens, while the whole city was full of fountains, supplied with pure water brought in pipes from the mountains round. I suppose so beautiful a sight as that city of Mexico has never been seen since on earth. Only one ugly feature there was in it—great pyramids of stone, hundreds of them, with idol temples on the top, on each of which was kept up a perpetual fire, fed with the fat of human beings.

To their surprise the Emperor received them peaceably, came out to meet them, gave them such presents, that the common soldiers were covered with chains of gold; invited them into the city, and gave them a magnificent palace to live in, and endless slaves to wait upon them. It sounds all like a fairy tale; but it is as true as that you and I are here.

But the cunning emperor had been plotting against them all the while; and no great blame to him; and at last one of those plots came to light; and Cortez made up his mind to take the Emperor prisoner. And he did it. Right or wrong, we can hardly say now. This Montezuma was a bad, false man, a tyrant and a cannibal; but still it looks ugly to seize a man who is acting as your friend. However, Cortez had courage, in the midst of that great city, with hundreds of thousands of Indians round him, to go and tell the Emperor that he must come with him. And—so strong is a man when he chooses to be strong—the Emperor actually went with Cortez a prisoner.

Cortez—and that was an unworthy action—put him in irons for an hour, to show him that he was master; and then took off his irons, and treated him like a king. The poor Emperor had all he wanted—all his wives, and slaves, and finery, and eatables, and drinkables; but he was a mere puppet in the Spaniard's hands; and knew it. And strangely enough, not being able to get out of his mind the fancy that these Spaniards were gods, or at least, the children of the gods, he treated them so generously and kindly, that they all loved him; he obeyed them in everything; took up a great friendship with several; and ended actually by giving them all his treasures of gold to melt down and part among themselves. As I say, it sounds all like a fairy tale, but it happened in this very month of November 1519.

But Cortez had been too prosperous not to meet with a mishap. Every great man must be tried by trouble; and so was Cortez. News came to him that a fresh army of Spaniards had landed, as he thought at first, to help him. They had nine hundred men, eighty of whom were horse soldiers, eighty musqueteers, one hundred and fifty cross-bow men, a good train of heavy guns, ammunition, &c. What was Cortez's disgust when he found that the treacherous Governor of Cuba had sent them, not to help him, but to take him prisoner as a rebel? It was a villainous business got up out of envy of Cortez's success, and covetousness of his booty. But in the Spanish colonies in those days, so far from home, there was very little law; and the governors and adventurers were always quarrelling and fighting with each other.

What did Cortez do? made up his mind as usual to do the desperate thing, and marched against Narvaez with only seventy men, no guns, and hardly any muskets—seventy against nine hundred. It was fearful odds; but he was forced to leave the rest to keep Mexico down. And he armed his men with very long lances, tipped at both ends with copper—for he had no iron; with them he hoped to face Narvaez's cavalry.

And he did it. Happily on his road he met an old friend with one hundred and twenty soldiers, who had been sent off to form a colony on the coast. They were as true as steel to him. And with that one hundred and ninety he surprised and defeated by night Narvaez's splendid little army. And what is more, after beating them, made such friends with them, that he engaged them all next morning to march with him wherever he wanted. The man was like a spider—whoever fell into his net, friend or foe, never came out again till he had sucked him dry.

Now he hurried back to Mexico, and terribly good reason he had; for Alvarado whom he had left in garrison had quarrelled with the Mexicans, and set upon them at one of their idol feasts, and massacred great numbers of their leading men. It was a bloody black business, and bitterly the Spaniards paid for it. Cortez when he heard it actually lost his temper for once, and called his lieutenant-general a madman and a traitor; but he could not afford to cashier him, for after all he was the best and bravest man he had. But the mischief was done. The whole city of Mexico, the whole country round, had risen in fury, had driven the Spanish garrison into the great palace; and worst of all, had burnt the boats, which Cortez had left to get off by, if the bridges were burst down. So there was Alvarado shut up, exactly like the English at Lucknow, with this difference, that the Spaniards deserved what they got, and the English, God knows, did not. And there was Cortez like another Havelock or Colin Campbell marching to deliver them. But he met a very different reception. These crafty Mexicans never struck a blow. All was as still as the grave. As they came over the long causeways and bridges, there was not a canoe upon the lake, not an Indian in the floating gardens. As they marched through the streets of the glorious city, the streets were as empty as a desert. And the Spaniard knew that he was walking into a trap, out of which none of them might come out alive; but their hearts never failed them, and they marched on to the sound of their bugles, and were answered by joyful salutes of cannon from the relieved garrison.

The Mexicans had shut up the markets, and no food was to be got. Cortez sent to open them. He sent another messenger off to the coast to say all was safe, and that he should soon conquer the rebels. But here, a cleverer man than I must tell the story.

"But scarcely had his messenger been gone half an hour, when he returned breathless with terror and covered with wounds. 'The city,' he said, 'was all in arms! the drawbridges were raised, and the enemy would soon be upon them! He spoke truth. It was not long before a hoarse sullen sound became audible, like that of the roaring of distant waters. It grew louder and louder, till from the parapet surrounding the enclosure, the great avenues which led to it might be seen dark with the masses of warriors, who came rolling on in a confused tide towards the fortress. At the same time the terraces and flat roofs in the neighbourhood were thronged with combatants, brandishing their missiles, who seemed to have risen up as if by magic! It was a spectacle to appall the stoutest. The Spanish forces were crowded into a small compact mass in the palace, and the whole army could be assembled at a moment's notice. No sooner, therefore, did the trumpet call to arms, than every soldier was at his post—the cavalry mounted, the artillerymen at their guns, and the archers and arquebusiers stationed so as to give the assailants a warm reception. On they came, with the companies, or irregular masses, into which the multitude was divided, rushing forward each in its own dense column, with many a gay banner displayed, and many a bright gleam of light reflected from helmet, arrow, and spear head, as they were tossed about in their disorderly array. As they drew near, the Aztecs set up a hideous yell, which rose far above the sound of shell and atabat, and their other rude instruments of warlike melody. They followed this by a tempest of missiles—stones, darts, arrows—which fell thick as rain on the besieged. The Spaniards waited till the foremost column had arrived, when a general discharge of artillery and arquebusses swept the ranks of the assailants, and mowed them down by hundreds."[4]...

So the fight raged on with fury for two days, while the Aztecs, Indians who only fought by day, howled out to the wretched Spaniards every night. On the third day Cortez brought out the Emperor Montezuma, and commanded him to quiet the Indians. The unhappy man obeyed him. He had made up his mind that these Spaniards were the white gods, who were to take his kingdom from him, and he submitted to them like a sheep to the butcher. He went up to a tower in all his royal robes and jewels. At the sight the Indians who filled the great square below were all hushed—thousands threw themselves on their faces; and to their utter astonishment, he asked them what they meant by rebelling. He was no prisoner, he said, but the Spaniard's guest and friend. The Spaniards would go peaceably, if they would let them. In any case he was the Spaniard's friend.

The Indians answered him by a yell of fury and contempt. He was a dog—a woman—fit only to weave and spin; and a volley of stones and arrows flew at him. One struck him on the head and dropped him senseless. The Indians set up a howl of terror; and frightened at what they had done, fled away ashamed.

The wretched Emperor refused comfort, food, help, tore the bandages from his wounds, and died in two days. He had been a bad man, a cannibal, and a butcher, blood-thirsty and covetous, a ravisher of virgins, and a tyrant to his people. But the Spaniards had got to love him in spite of all; for a true friend he had been to them, and a fearful loss to them just now. The battle went on worse than ever. The great idol temple commanded the palace, and was covered with Mexican warriors. And next day Cortez sent a party to storm it. They tried to get up the winding stairs, and were driven back three times with fearful loss. Cortez, though he had but one hand to fight with, sallied out and cleared the pyramid himself, after a fearful hand-to-hand fight of three hours, up the winding stairs, along the platforms, and at last upon the great square on the top, an acre in breadth. Every Mexican was either killed, or hurled down the sides. The idol, the war god, with its gold disc of bleeding hearts smoking before it, was hurled down and the whole accursed place set on fire and destroyed. Three hundred houses round were also burnt that night; but of what use?

The Spaniards were starving, hemmed in by hundreds of thousands. They were like a single wasp inside a bee-hive. Let him kill the bees by hundreds, he must be killed himself at last. He

---

4 Prescott's "History of the Conquest of Mexico." See Book v., ch. 1.

made up his mind to evacuate the city, to leave all his conquests behind him. It was a terrible disappointment, but it had to be done.

They marched out by night in good order, with all their guns and ammunition, and with immense plunder; as much of poor Montezuma's treasures as they could carry. The old hands took very little; they knew what they were about. The fresh ones from Narvaez's army loaded themselves with gold and jewels, and had to pay dear for them. Cortez, I ought to tell you, took good care of Dona Marina. He sent her forward under a strong guard of Tlascalans, with all the other women. The great street was crossed by many canals. Then the causeway across the lake, two miles long, was crossed by more canals, and at every one of these the Indians had taken away the bridges. Cortez knew that, and had made a movable bridge; but he had only time to make one, and that of course had to be taken up at the rear, and carried forward to the front every time they crossed a dyke; and that made endless delay. As long as they were in the city, however, all went well; but the moment they came out upon the lake causeway, out thundered the serpent-skin drums from the top of every temple, the conch shells blew, and out swarmed the whole hive of bees, against the one brave wasp who was struggling. The Spaniards cleared the dyke by cavalry and artillery, and got to the first canal, laid down the bridge, and over slowly but safely, amid a storm of stones and arrows. They got to the second canal, fifteen or twenty feet broad. Why, in God's name, was not the bridge brought on? Instead of the bridge came news from the rear. The weight of the artillery had been too great for the bridge, and it was jammed fast. And there they were on a narrow dyke fifty feet broad, in the midst of the lake, in the dark midnight, with countless thousands of Indians, around, before, behind, and the lord have mercy on them!

What followed you may guess—though some of the brave men who fought there, and who wrote the story themselves—which I have read—hardly knew.

The cavalry tried to swim their horses over. Some got safe, others rolled into the lake. The infantry followed pell mell, cut down like sheep by arrows and stones, by the terrible glass swords of the Indians, who crowded round their canoes. The waggons prest on the men, the guns on them, the rear on them again, till in a few minutes the canal was choked with writhing bodies of men and horses, cannon, gold and treasure inestimable, over which the survivors scrambled to the further bank. Cortez, who was helping the rear forded the gap on horseback, and hurried on to find a third and larger canal which no one dare cross. But the Indians were not so thick here, and plunging into the water they got through as they could. And woe that night to the soldier who had laden himself with Indian treasure. Dragged to the bottom by the weight of their plunder, hundreds died there drowned by that very gold to find which they had crossed the seas, and fought so many a bloody battle.

What is the use of making a sad story long? They reached the shore, and sat down like men desperate and foredone in a great idol temple. Several of their finest officers, three-fourths of their men, were killed and missing, three-fourths too of their horses—all Cortez's papers, all their cannon, all their treasure. They had not even a musket left. Nothing to face the Indians with but twenty-three crippled horses, a few damaged crossbows, and their good old swords. Cortez's first question was for poor Dona Marima, and strange to say she was safe. The trusty Tlascalan Indians had brought her through it all. Alvarado the lieutenant was safe too. If he had been the cause of all that misery, he did his best to make up for it. He stayed behind fighting at the last canal till all were over, and the Indians closing round him. Then he set his long lance in the water, and to the astonishment of both armies, leapt the canal clean, while the Indians shouted, "This is indeed the Tonatiah, the child of the Sun." The gap is shown now, and it is called to this day, Alvarado's Leap. God forgive him! for if he was a cruel man, he was at least a brave one!

Cortez sat down, a ruined man, and as he looked round for his old comrades, and missed one face after another, he covered his face with his hands and cried like a child.

And was he a ruined man? Never less. No man is ruined till his pluck is gone. He got his starving and shivering men together, and away for the mountains to get back to the friendly people of Tlascala. The people followed them along the hills shouting, "Go on! you will soon find yourselves where you cannot escape." But he went on—till he saw what they meant.

Waiting for him in a pass was an army of Indians—two hundred thousand, some writers say—all fresh and fully armed. What could he do? To surrender, was to be sacrificed every man to the idols; so he marched on. He had still twenty horses, and he put ten on each flank. He bade his men not strike with their sword but give the point. He made a speech to his men. They had beaten the Indians, he said, many a time at just as fearful odds. God had brought them through so far, God would not desert them, for they were fighting on His side against the heathen; and so he went straight at the vast army of Indians. They were surrounded, swallowed up by them for a few minutes. In the course of an hour the Spaniards had routed them utterly with immense slaughter.

Of all the battles I ever read of, this battle of Otumba is one of the most miraculous. Some say that Cortez conquered Mexico by gunpowder: he had none then, neither cannon nor musket. The sword and lance did it all, and they in the hands of men worn out with famine, cold, and fatigue, and I had said broken-hearted into the bargain. But there was no breaking those men's hearts—what won that battle, what won Mexico, was the indomitable pluck of the white man, before which the Indian, whether American or Hindoo, never has stood, and never will stand to the world's end. The Spaniards proved it in America of old, though they were better armed than the Indian. But there are those who have proved it upon Indians as well armed as themselves. Ay, my friends, I should be no Englishman, if while I told this story, I could help thinking all the while of our brave comrades in India, who have conquered as Cortez conquered, and against just as fearful odds; whose enemies were armed, not with copper arrows and glass knives, but with European muskets, European cannon, and most dangerous of all, European discipline. I say Cortez did wonders in his time; but I say too that our Indian heroes have done more, and done it in a better cause.

And that is the history of the conquest of Mexico. What, you may ask, is that the end? When we are leaving the Spaniards a worn-out and starving handful struggling back for refuge to Tlascala, without anything but their old swords; do you call that a conquest?

Yes, I do; just as I call the getting back to Cawnpore, after the relief of Lucknow, the conquest of India. It showed which was the better man, Englishman or sepoy, just as the retreat from Mexico showed which was the better man, Spaniard or Indian. The sepoys were cowed from that day, just as the Mexicans were cowed after Otumba. They had fought with all possible odds on their side, and been licked; and when men are once cowed, all the rest is merely a work of time.

So it was with Cortez. He went back to Tlascala. He got by mere accident, as we say, a reinforcement of Spaniards. He stirred up all the Indian nations round, who were weary of the cruel tyranny of the Mexicans; he made large boats to navigate the lake, and he marched back upon Mexico the next year with about six hundred Spaniards and nine cannon—about half the force which he had had before; but with a hundred thousand Indian allies, who, like the sturdy Tlascalans, proved as true to him as steel. Truly, if he was not a great general, who is?

He marched back, taking city after city as he went, and besieged Mexico. It was a long and weary siege. The Indians fought like fiends. The causeways had to be taken yard by yard; but Cortez, wise by sad experience, put his cannon into the boats and swept them from the water. Then the city had to be taken house by house. The Indians drove him back again and again, till they were starved to skeletons, and those who used to eat their enemies were driven to eat each other. Still they would not give in. At last, after many weeks of fighting, it was all over. The glorious Mexican empire was crumbled to dust. Those proud nobles, who used to fat themselves upon the bodies of all the nations round, were reduced to a handful of starving beggars. The cross of Christ was set up, where the hearts of human creatures were offered to foul idols, and Mexico has been ever since the property of the Spaniards, a Christian land.

And what became of Cortez? He died sadly and in disgrace. He sowed, and other men reaped. If he was cruel and covetous, he was punished for it in this world heavily enough. He had many noble qualities though. He was a better man than those around him; and one good thing he did, which was to sweep off the face of the earth as devilish a set of tyrants as ever defiled the face of the earth. Give him all due honour for it, and let him rest in peace. God shall judge him and not we.

But take home with you, soldiers all, one lesson from this strange story, that while a man can keep his courage and his temper, he is not only never really beaten, but no man can tell what great things he may not do.

III

PICTURE GALLERIES

Picture-galleries should be the working-man's paradise,[5] a garden of pleasure, to which he goes to refresh his eyes and heart with beautiful shapes and sweet colouring, when they are wearied with dull bricks and mortar, and the ugly colourless things which fill the town, the workshop and the factory. For, believe me, there is many a road into our hearts besides our ears and brains; many a sight, and sound, and scent, even, of which we have never thought at all, sinks into our memory, and helps to shape our characters; and thus children brought up among beautiful sights and sweet sounds will most likely show the fruits of their nursing, by thoughtfulness and affection, and nobleness of mind, even by the expression of the countenance. The poet Wordsworth, talking of training up a beautiful country girl, says:—

"The floating clouds their state shall lend
To her—for her the willow bend;
Nor shall she fail to see,
Even in the motions of the storm,
Grace which shall mould the maiden's form,
By silent sympathy.

* * * * *

And she shall bend her ear
In many a secret place
Where rivulets dance their wayward round,
And beauty, born of murmuring sound,
Shall pass into her face."

Those who live in towns should carefully remember this, for their own sakes, for their wives' sakes, for their children's sakes. Never lose an opportunity of seeing anything beautiful. Beauty is

---

5 Mr. Kingsley wrote these papers for London working-men, but his words apply just as much to soldiers in London barracks, as to artizans. He thought much of the good of pictures, and all beautiful things for hard-worked men who could see such things in public galleries, though they could not afford to have them in their own homes.

God's handwriting—a wayside sacrament; welcome it in every fair face, every fair sky, every fair flower, and thank Him for it, who is the fountain of all loveliness, and drink it in, simply and earnestly, with all your eyes; it is a charmed draught, a cup of blessing.

Therefore I said that picture-galleries should be the townsman's paradise of refreshment. Of course, if he can get the real air, the real trees, even for an hour, let him take it, in God's name; but how many a man who cannot spare time for a daily country walk, may well slip into the National Gallery in Trafalgar Square (or the South Kensington Museum), or any other collection of pictures, for ten minutes. That garden, at least, flowers as gaily in winter as in summer. Those noble faces on the wall are never disfigured by grief or passion. There, in the space of a single room, the townsman may take his country walk—a walk beneath mountain peaks, blushing sunsets, with broad woodlands spreading out below it; a walk through green meadows, under cool mellow shades, and overhanging rocks, by rushing brooks, where he watches and watches till he seems to hear the foam whisper, and to see the fishes leap; and his hard worn heart wanders out free, beyond the grim city-world of stone and iron, smoky chimneys, and roaring wheels, into the world of beautiful things—the world which shall be hereafter—ay, which shall be! Believe it, toil-worn worker, in spite of thy foul alley, thy crowded lodging, thy grimed clothing, thy ill-fed children, thy thin, pale wife—believe it, thou too and thine, will some day have your share of beauty. God made you love beautiful things only because He intends hereafter to give you your fill of them. That pictured face on the wall is lovely, but lovelier still may the wife of thy bosom be when she meets thee on the resurrection morn! Those baby cherubs in the old Italian painting—how gracefully they flutter and sport among the soft clouds, full of rich young life and baby joy! Yes, beautiful indeed, but just such a one at this very moment is that once pining, deformed child of thine, over whose death-cradle thou wast weeping a month ago; now a child-angel, whom thou shalt meet again never to part! Those landscapes, too, painted by loving, wise old Claude, two hundred years ago, are still as fresh as ever. How still the meadows are! how pure and free that vault of deep blue sky! No wonder that thy worn heart, as thou lookest, sighs aloud, "Oh that I had wings as a dove, then would I flee away and be at rest." Ah, but gayer meadows and bluer skies await thee in the world to come—that fairy-land made real—"the new heavens and the new earth," which God has prepared for the pure and the loving, the just and the brave, who have conquered in this sore fight of life!

These thoughts may seem all too far-fetched to spring up in a man's head from merely looking at pictures; but it is not so in practice. See, now, such thoughts have sprung up in my head; how else did I write them down here? And why should not they, and better ones, too, spring up in your heads, friends? It is delightful to watch in a picture-gallery some street-boy enjoying himself; how first wonder creeps over his rough face, and then a sweeter, more earnest, awestruck look, till his countenance seems to grow handsomer and nobler on the spot, and drink in and reflect unknowingly, the beauty of the picture he is studying. See how some soldier's face will light up before the painting which tells him a noble story of bye-gone days. And why? Because he feels as if he himself had a share in the story at which he looks. They may be noble and glorious men who are painted there; but they are still men of like passions with himself, and his man's heart understands them and glories in them; and he begins, and rightly, to respect himself the more when he finds that he, too, has a fellow-feeling with noble men and noble deeds.

I say, pictures raise blessed thoughts in me—why not in you, my brothers? Your hearts are fresh, thoughtful, kindly; you only want to have these pictures explained to you, that you may know why and how they are beautiful, and what feelings they ought to stir in your minds. Look at the portraits on the walls, and let me explain one or two. Often the portraits are simpler than large pictures, and they speak of real men and women who once lived on this earth of ours—generally of remarkable and noble men—and man should be always interesting to man.

IV

A PORTRAIT IN THE NATIONAL GALLERY

"Any one who goes to the National Gallery in Trafalgar Square, may see two large and beautiful pictures—the nearer of the two labelled 'Titian,' representing Bacchus leaping from a car drawn by leopards. The other, labelled 'Francia,' representing the Holy Family seated on a sort of throne, with several figures arranged below—one of them a man pierced with arrows. Between these two, low down, hangs a small picture, about two feet square, containing only the portrait of an old man, in a white cap and robe, and labelled on the picture itself, 'Joannes Bellinus.' Now this old man is a very ancient friend of mine, and has comforted my heart, and preached me a sharp sermon, too, many a time. I never enter that gallery without having five minutes' converse with him; and yet he has been dead at least three hundred years, and, what is more, I don't even know his name. But what more do I know of a man by knowing his name? Whether the man's name be Brown, or whether he has as many names and titles as a Spanish grandee, what does that tell me about the man?—the spirit and character of the man—what the man will say when he is asked—what the man will do when he is stirred up to action? The man's name is part of his clothes; his shell; his husk. Change his name and all his titles, you don't change him—'a man's a man for a' that,' as Burns says; and a goose a goose. Other men gave him his name; but his heart and his spirit—his love and his hatred—his wisdom and his folly—his power to do well and ill; those God and himself gave him. I must know those, and then I know the man. Let us see what we can make out from the picture itself about the man whom it represents. In the first place, we may see by his dress that he was in his day the Doge (or chief magistrate) of Venice—the island city, the queen of the seas. So we may guess that he had many a stirring time of it, and many a delicate game to play among those tyrannous and covetous old merchant-princes who had elected him; who were keeping up their own power at the expense of everyone's liberty, by spies and nameless accusers, and secret councils, tortures, and prisons, whose horrors no one ever returned to describe. Nay, we may guess just the very men with whom he had to deal—the very battles he may have seen fought.

"But all these are circumstances—things which stand round the man (as the word means), and not the whole man himself—not the character and heart of the man: that we must get from the portrait; and if the portrait is a truly noble portrait we shall get it. If it is a merely vulgar picture, we shall get the man's dress and shape of his face, but little or no expression: if it is a pathetic portrait, or picture of passion, we shall get one particular temporary expression of his face—perhaps joy, sorrow, anger, disgust—but still one which may have passed any moment, and left his face quite different; but if the picture is one of the noblest kind, we shall read the man's whole character there; just all his strength and weakness, his kindliness or his sternness, his thoughtfulness or his carelessness, written there once and for ever;—what he would be, though all the world passed away; what his immortal and eternal soul will be, unless God or the devil changed his heart, to all eternity.

"We may see at once that this man has been very handsome; but it is a peculiar sort of beauty. How delicate and graceful all the lines in his face are!—he is a gentleman of God's own making, and not of the tailor's making. He is such a gentleman as I have seen among working men and nine-shilling-a-week labourers, often and often; his nobleness is in his heart—it is God's gift, therefore it shows in his noble looking face. No matter whether he were poor or rich; all the rags in the world, all the finery in the world, could not have made him look like a snob or a swell. He was a thoughtful man, too; no one with such a forehead could have been a trifler: a kindly man, too, and honest—one that may have played merrily enough with his grandchildren, and put his hand in his purse for many a widow and orphan. Look what a bright, clear, straightforward, gentle look he has, almost a smile; but he has gone through too many sad hours to smile much: he is a man of many sorrows, like all true and noble rulers; and, like a high mountain-side, his face bears the furrows of many storms. He has had a stern life of it, with the cares of a great nation on his shoulders. He has seen that in this world there is no rest for those who live like true men: you may see it by the wrinkles in his brow, and the sharp-cut furrows in his cheeks, and those firm-set, determined lips. His eyes almost show the marks of many noble tears,—tears such as good men shed over their nation's sins; but that, too, is past now. He has found out his path, and he will keep it; and he has no misgiving now about what God would have him do, or about the reward which God has laid up for the brave and just; and that is what makes his forehead so clear and bright, while his very teeth are clenched with calm determination. And by the look of those high cheek bones, and that large square jaw, he is a strong-willed man enough, and not one to be easily turned aside from his purpose by any man alive, or by any woman either, or by his own passions and tempers. One fault of character, I think, he may perhaps have had much trouble with—I mean bitterness and contemptuousness. His lips are very thin; he may have sneered many a time, when he was younger, at the follies of the world which that great, lofty, thoughtful brain and clear eye of his told him were follies; but he seems to have got past that too. Such is the man's character: a noble, simple, commanding old man, who has conquered many hard things, and, hardest of all, has conquered himself, and now is waiting calm for his everlasting rest. God send us all the same.

"Now consider the deep insight of old John Bellini, who could see all this, and put it down there for us with pencil and paint. No doubt there was something in Bellini's own character which made him especially best able to paint such a man; for we always understand those who are most like ourselves; and therefore you may tell pretty nearly a painter's own character by seeing what sort of subjects he paints, and what his style of painting is. And a noble, simple, brave, godly man was old John Bellini, who never lost his head, though princes were flattering him and snobs following him with shouts and blessings for his noble pictures of the Venetian victories, as if he had been a man sent from God Himself, as indeed he was—all great painters are; for who but God makes beauty? Who gives the loving heart, and the clear eye, and the graceful taste to see beauty and to copy it, and to set forth on canvas, or in stone, the noble deeds of patriots dying for their country? To paint truly patriotic pictures well, a man must have his heart in his work—he must be a true patriot himself, as John Bellini was (if I mistake not, he had fought for his country himself in more than one shrewd fight). And what makes men patriots, or artists, or anything noble at all, but the spirit of the living God? Those great pictures of Bellini's are no more; they were burnt a few years afterwards, with the magnificent national hall in which they hung; but the spirit of them is not passed away. Even now, Venice, Bellini's beloved mother-land, is rising, new-born, from long weary years of Austrian slavery, and trying to be free and great once more; and young Italian hearts are lighting up with the thoughts of her old fleets and her old victories, her merchants and her statesmen, whom John Bellini drew. Venice sinned, and fell; and sorely has she paid for her sins, through two hundred years of shame, and profligacy, and slavery. And she has broken the oppressor's yoke. God send her a new life! May she learn by her ancient sins! May she learn by her ancient glories!

"You will forgive me for forgetting my picture to talk of such things. But we must return. Look back at what I said about the old portrait—the clear, calm, victorious character of the old man's face, and see how all the rest of the picture agrees with it, in a complete harmony. The dress, the scenery, the light and shade, the general 'tone' of colour should all agree with the character of the face—all help to bring our minds into that state in which we may best feel and sympathise with the human beings painted. Now here, because the face is calm and grand, the colour and the outlines are quiet and grand likewise. How different these colours are from that glorious 'Holy Family' of Francia's, next to it on the right; or from that equally glorious 'Bacchus and Ariadne' of Titian's, on the left! Yet all three are right, each for its own subject. Here you have no brilliant reds, no rich warm browns; no luscious greens. The white robe and cap give us the thought of purity and simplicity; the very golden embroidery on them, which marks his rank, is carefully kept back from being too gaudy. Everything is sober here; and the lines of the dress, how simple they all are—no rich curves, no fluttering drapery. They would be quite stiff if it were not for that waving line of round tassels in front, which break the extreme straightness and heaviness of the splendid robe; and all pointing upwards towards that solemn, thin, calm face, with its high white cap, rising like the peak of a snow mountain against the dark, deep, boundless blue sky beyond. That is a grand thought of Bellini's. You do not see the man's hands; he does not want them now, his work is done. You see no landscape behind—no buildings. All earth's ways and sights are nothing to him now; there is nothing but the old man and the sky—nothing between him and the heaven now, and he knows it and is glad. A few months more, and those way-worn features shall have crumbled to their dust, and that strong, meek spirit shall be in the abyss of eternity, before the God from whence it came.

"So says John Bellini, with art more cunning than words. And if this paper shall make one of you look at that little picture with fresh interest, and raise one strong and solemn longing in you to die the death of the righteous, and let your last end be like his who is painted there—then I shall rejoice in the only payment I desire to get, for this my afternoon's writing."

V

THE BRITISH MUSEUM

Nature is infinitely more wonderful than the highest art; and in the commonest hedgeside leaf lies a mystery and beauty greater than that of the greatest picture, the noblest statue—as infinitely greater as God's work is infinitely greater than man's. But to those who have no leisure to study nature in the green fields (and there are now-a-days too many such, though the time may come when all will have that blessing), to such I say, go to the British Museum, Bloomsbury Square; there at least, if you cannot go to nature's wonders, some of nature's wonders are brought to you.

The British Museum is my glory and joy; because it is one of the only places which is free to English citizens as such—where the poor and the rich may meet together, and before those works of God's Spirit, "who is no respecter of persons," feel that "the Lord is the maker of them all." In the British Museum and the National Gallery, the Englishman may say, "Whatever my coat or my purse, I am an Englishman, and therefore I have a right here. I can glory in these noble halls, as if they were my own house."

English commerce, the joint enterprise and industry of the poor sailor as well as the rich merchant, brought home these treasures from foreign lands; and those glorious statues—though it was the wealth and taste of English noblemen and gentlemen (who in that proved themselves truly noble and gentle) who placed them here, yet it was the genius of English artists—men at once above and below all ranks—men who have worked their way up, not by money or birth, but by worth and genius, which taught the noble and wealthy the value of those antiques, and which proclaimed their beauty to the world. The British Museum is a truly equalising place, in the deepest and most spiritual sense. And it gives the lie, too, to that common slander, "that the English are not worthy of free admission to valuable and curious collections, because they have such a trick of seeing with their fingers; such a trick of scribbling their names, of defiling and disfiguring works of art. On the Continent it may do, but you cannot trust the English."

This has been, like many other untruths, so often repeated, that people now take it for granted; but I believe that it is utterly groundless, and I say so on the experience of the British Museum and the National Gallery. In the only two cases, I believe, in which injury has been done to anything in either place, the destroyers were neither working-men, nor even poor reckless heathen street-boys, but persons who had received what is too often miscalled "a liberal education." But national property will always be respected, because all will be content, while they feel that they have their rights, and all will be careful while they feel that they have a share in the treasure.

Go to the British Museum in Easter week, and see there hundreds of thousands, of every rank and age, wandering past sculptures and paintings, which would be ruined by a blow—past jewels and curiosities, any one of which would buy many a poor soul there a month's food and lodging—only protected by a pane of glass, if by that; and then see not a thing disfigured—much less stolen. Everywhere order, care, attention, honest pride in their country's wealth and science; earnest reverence for the mighty works of God, and of the God-inspired. I say, the people of England prove themselves worthy of free admission to all works of art, and it is therefore the duty of those who can to help them to that free admission.

What a noble, and righteous, and truly brotherly plan it would be, if all classes would join to form a free National Gallery of Art and Science, which might combine the advantages of the present Polytechnic, Society of Arts, and British Institution, gratis.[6] Manufacturers and men of science might send thither specimens of their new inventions. The rich might send, for a few months in the year—as they do now to the British Institution—ancient and modern pictures, and not only pictures, but all sorts of curious works of art and nature, which are now hidden in their drawing-rooms and libraries. There might be free liberty to copy any object, on the copyist's name and residence being registered. And surely artists and men of science might be found, with enough of the spirit of patriotism and love, to explain gratuitously to all comers, whatever their rank or class, the wonders of the Museum. I really believe that if once the spirit of brotherhood got abroad among us; if men once saw that here was a vast means of educating, and softening and uniting those who have no leisure for study, and few means of enjoyment, except the gin-shop and Cremorne Gardens; if they could but once feel that here was a project, equally blessed for rich and poor, the money for it would be at once forthcoming from many a rich man, who is longing to do good, if he could only be shown the way; and from many a poor journeyman, who would gladly

---

[6] Since this paper was written in 1848 many such institutions have been opened, at South Kensington, and in several great towns.

contribute his mite to a truly national museum. All that is wanted is the spirit of self-sacrifice, patriotism and brotherly love—which God alone can give—which I believe He is giving more and more in these very days.

I never felt this more strongly than one day, as I was looking in at the windows of a splendid curiosity-shop in Oxford Street, at a case of humming-birds. I was gloating over the beauty of those feathered jewels, and then wondering what was the meaning, what was the use of it all? why those exquisite little creatures should have been hidden for ages, in all their splendours of ruby, and emerald, and gold in the South American forests, breeding and fluttering and dying, that some dozen out of all those millions might be brought over here to astonish the eyes of men. And as I asked myself, why were all these boundless varieties, these treasures of unseen beauty, created? my brain grew dizzy between pleasure and thought; and, as always happens when one is most innocently delighted, "I turned to share the joy," as Wordsworth says; and next to me stood a huge, brawny coal-heaver, in his shovel hat, and white stockings and high-lows, gazing at the humming-birds as earnestly as myself. As I turned he turned, and I saw a bright manly face, with a broad, soot-grimmed forehead, from under which a pair of keen flashing eyes gleamed wondering, smiling sympathy into mine. In that moment we felt ourselves friends. If we had been Frenchmen, we should, I suppose, have rushed into each other's arms and "fraternised" upon the spot. As we were a pair of dumb, awkward Englishmen, we only gazed a half-minute, staring into each other's eyes, with a delightful feeling of understanding each other, and then burst out both at once with, "Isn't that beautiful?" "Well, that is!" And then both turned back again, to stare at our humming-birds.

I never felt more thoroughly than at that minute (though, thank God, I had often felt it before) that all men were brothers; that this was not a mere political doctrine, but a blessed God-ordained fact; that the party-walls of rank and fashion and money were but a paper prison of our own making, which we might break through any moment by a single hearty and kindly feeling; that the one spirit of God was given without respect of persons; that the beautiful things were beautiful alike to the coal-heaver and the parson; and that before the wondrous works of God and of God's inspired genius, the rich and the poor might meet together, and feel that whatever the coat or the creed may be, "A man's a man for a' that," and one Lord the maker of them all.

For, believe me, my friends, rich and poor—and I beseech you to think deeply over this great truth—that men will never be joined in true brotherhood by mere plans to give them a self-interest in common, as the Socialists have tried to do. No: to feel for each other, they must first feel with each other. To have their sympathies in common, they must have not one object of gain, but an object of admiration in common; to know that they are brothers, they must feel that they have one Father; and one way to feel that they have one common Father, is to see each other wondering, side by side, at His glorious works!

THE END

www.ingramcontent.com/pod-product-compliance
Ingram Content Group UK Ltd.
Pitfield, Milton Keynes, MK11 3LW, UK
UKHW012249290726
14090UKWH00013B/547

9 798888 309582